Soccer Drills

ALSO BY ALBERT M. LUONGO:

*The Soccer Handbook
for Players, Coaches and Parents*
(McFarland, 1996)

Soccer Drills

Skill-Builders
for Field Control

by
ALBERT M. LUONGO

...nd & Company, Inc., Publishers
...n, North Carolina, and London

Library of Congress Cataloguing-in-Publication Data

Luongo, Albert M., 1939–
    Soccer drills : skill-builders for field control / by Albert M. Luongo.
      p.   cm.
    Includes index.

    ISBN-13: 978-0-7864-0682-1
    (softcover : 50# alkaline paper) ∞

    1. Soccer—Training.   I. Title.

  GV943.9.T7 L86   2000
  796.334'2—dc21   99-47698

British Library Cataloguing-in-Publication data are available

Manufactured in the United States of America

McFarland & Company, Inc., Publishers
  Box 611, Jefferson, North Carolina 28640
   www.mcfarlandpub.com

Contents

List of Figures
and Illustrations

Figures

Illustrations

Introduction

This book was written as a follow-up to *The Soccer Handbook for Players, Coaches and Parents*. I believe that meaningful drills will improve the quality of North American soccer.

I have spent many years intensively involved in every aspect of amateur soccer, from organizing a house league and traveling teams in Park Ridge, N.J., in 1977, to being a player-coach of adult soccer teams, to being a referee. I have been fortunate to manage and play alongside many highly skilled foreign-born players and managers, and I have selected the best of their time tested techniques in the form of progressive drills. Today's excellent soccer players have reached a sophisticated level only by realizing that there is no substitute for self-discipline and mastery of basic skills. To pass on this knowledge, I have incorporated their skills and wisdom.

Few young players get the full picture that this sport requires, including an understanding of how a team should function as a tightly organized unit. Coaches should emphasize to young players that teamwork is far more advantageous than individual play and that before true teamwork can develop, players must learn and apply basic skills. Only skillful players can understand their places in a team's structure, and structure is important for winning.

The individual drills in this book will then be used with plays involving several nearby players during games. For instance, early drills such as passing, trapping, shielding and individual defending will eventually merge in later drills such as the Goalkeeping Defense Drill (Drill 3.7) or the Halfback and Wing Overlap with Shot Drill (Drill 6.8). Naturally, these later offensive and defensive teamwork drills will be effective only if the basic skills have taken hold. Even though a greater percentage of the drills in this book promote attacking skills than defensive skills, proper defense is paramount to winning and is highly stressed.

The drills for individual skills are in a relatively tight sequence and because they are requisite to the advanced teammate drills that follow, it is strongly recommended that this sequence be followed.

Although there are very few set plays in soccer, this book will refer to frequently repeated field conditions as "plays." Similar situations recur

1

repeatedly, and players need to recognize them to take advantage of every opportunity. In such opportunities they can make good use of the plays taught in the drills, and can utilize teammates to overpower opponents that may still be playing on an individual basis.

Skillful team play comes about in later drills via a buildup of individual skills developed earlier, but to be winners your players must have not only an overall knowledge of the game and mastery of individual skills but also the stamina and understanding to perform these skills under pressure.

This handbook promotes a specific style known as short ball soccer. This is a game where the ball is controlled at ground level most of the time, minimizing such techniques as long, high kicks, and heading. The style of play recommended here is different from the long ball type of game where the ball is in the air most of the time, moved ahead by long air passes to the forward players. For the non-skilled, this type of play results in a game of kickball. The short-ball version of the game requires more control and is more effective.

This drill book is thus aimed at promoting a better type of soccer than is generally played at the amateur levels in North America. Short ball is the type of soccer played by the top competitive teams of the world and is seen in the playoffs in World Cup soccer. It is the soccer that comes out of countries such as Argentina, Brazil, Germany, Italy, some African countries and a few others, but it can also be seen in some North American professional soccer games. It is my observation that up until several years ago, top German teams played long ball soccer, but after numerous defeats by South American teams, they rapidly switched to the short ball game. This was a good decision.

To produce an excellent soccer team or league, the scoring of goals must not be the focus of all activities. Skillful defensive knowledge and a well implemented plan enabling players to develop skills provide the best chance of success. In other words, sound methods should be routine. Success is not easy to come by nor is it achieved quickly. Prudent training measures must be installed and adhered to and this takes a constant commitment on everyone's part. It takes time, foresight and self-discipline.

A way to promote top class soccer is through the adaptation of a club charter. With such a charter, conditions such as coaches' training, referees' training, and ongoing evaluations would follow. The goal would be eventually to eliminate outdated soccer methods, poor refereeing and poor coaching. Better soccer is a game where both teams control both themselves and the ball with purposeful play and with a reduced emphasis on the intimidation-by-roughness methods practiced by some unskillful teams or youth leagues.

At the team level, each player and age group should be receiving the same training message. The basics must be learned and each player has a particular function on the team. If all players are trained in a certain playing style, they know what to expect. When each player on the team is performing his or her duties properly and in accordance with training methods, the conditions are set for certain individuals to become creative. But if the players are getting mixed messages—for example, if they receive instructions in training drills that are contradicted in games or by other coaches—the players will be confused, have less respect for coaches and management, and will never play at an optimum level. Consistency, uniformity of methods, and policy must be adhered to.

Young players must be allowed to try out the practiced techniques and make mistakes in games in order for them to learn and play in a consistent manner. In fact, coaches should insist that players try out the practiced techniques in real game situations. If the principles taught through the drills in this book are embedded in young players' minds and muscles, they will be on their way to playing top class soccer.

Top class soccer is a game of control (usually by both teams) and minimization of errors. This is opposed to the uncontrolled, haphazard soccer of unskilled players. Awareness of unskillful play is the first step towards the attainment of a higher level soccer.

Here are some game activities that signal unskillful play:

- Players indiscriminately kicking and head or foot flicking the ball up field to gain yardage.
- Defense attacking the ball in an attempt to dislodge it from opponents.
- Players kicking or heading the ball far up field.
- Throw-ins up the line (opposition players ordinarily gather at this point on the field).
- Players keeping the ball nearly constantly in the air.
- Players frequently sending the ball over the touch or end lines.
- Players engaging in rough play or causing many penalties.
- Goalkeeper constantly kicking the ball up field.
- Goalkeeper taking too much time to restart the play.

- One or more players hanging back when goal kicks are taken.
- Kick-offs that immediately press the ball forward into the opposition.
- Very little trapping.
- Few passes that can be controlled by teammates.
- Many long shots on goal or nearly 90 degree angled shots on goal from the corner.

These activities indicate little control on the field. If any of the above exist, some (perhaps much) remedial training is necessary to upgrade your soccer team or league with ground-level skills.

Changes will not come easily. A coach cannot just toss basic skills into the repertoire of older players. Regardless of age or experience, players must go back to square one and repetitiously build elementary skills, not simply be shown how to use them and they must train with these skills without being tempted to mix in advanced skills—advanced skills depend upon basics that may not be in place.

The drills in this book are effective only if they are continuously utilized. If the basics are taught only for a short time and other techniques are introduced prematurely, skillful soccer will not result. In order for players to develop, a league must require and enforce skillful training methods and ensure that all coaches are in synch with a league's or club's expectations.

For the most part, the results of these drills will not be apparent for quite some time. Furthermore, the application of these drills will not in itself produce great players, as skillful play is but one ingredient. To be in a top class, a player must be well balanced and possess other important attributes apart from technical skill. These include the ability to compete against other excellent players through endurance developed from off-the-field running; a keen mind and honest self-assessment; modesty; leadership; teamwork that makes other players look good; and—very importantly—an aggressive spirit to win the loose ball.

I am presenting only guidelines for drills that simulate normal situations that occur in soccer matches. Coaches and managers should use this book only as a guide. Common sense must be employed in the use of these drills. If any of them are not quite understood or seem too harsh, injurious or harmful in any way to any of the participants, they should be discarded.

Because soccer is a sport requiring much endurance, it is strongly recommended that all participants be examined by medical professionals before the soccer season begins as well as during the season.

The soccer style presented in this text calls for a minimal use of the head to propel or to trap the ball. If any parent or player does not want the head to be so employed, other trapping skills can be used as a substitute in most situations.

The Illustrations and Figures

Throughout this book, "figures" depict drills, while "illustrations" depict fine points of technique.

In the figures, the broken-line circle shows the initial position of the ball. The solid circle is the final position of the ball, located at the arrow tip.

Many of the figures contain insets, called stages. They depict movements of the players as the drill progresses.

1. Background for the Drills

In order to understand the purpose of the drills, an overview is necessary. Some of the topics were briefly discussed in the Introduction, but will now be presented in greater detail.

On Soccer Organizations

Soccer leagues should promote the best and most modern form of soccer, but this is not always the case. Leagues are generally formed for purposes of casual recreation and, generally, little time is dedicated to maximizing players' skills. This is natural, as it takes an enormous effort just to coordinate games, practice sessions and associated activities. Most leagues grow and evolve. Some evolve into strong and fair organizations while others grow in membership, but remain weak and political. Weak clubs or leagues may lose sight of the founders' ideals. It should, just for instance, be a major concern when coaches frequently contradict their own training methods during game play.

The objective of all clubs and leagues should be a strong and permanent organization for the players' benefit. One way to achieve it is by setting higher standards for skills and fairness. Today's young players will become tomorrow's leaders applying the good or bad leadership principals learned in their youth. The development of a young athlete's potential does not come about haphazardly: We know from televised Olympic training methods that the conditioning of athletes can be both scientific and thorough. Olympic hopefuls generally do not employ just any coach, but teams of experts. Soccer, at the youth level, should be similar.

Your child's training should be with coaches who know correct methods and who promote fairness. Many coaches may not be well trained in coaching—but they could be and should be. Soccer organizations should take on the responsibility to train coaches prior to a season, using a selected and experienced senior coach. The club or league should have the last word on just when and how young players are to be taught basic skills. They should also have procedures for resolving complaints and conflicts. In addition, each soccer club and league should continually examine itself if it wishes to improve the level of play and the organization's health. As part of their weekly business these organizations should have the following on the agenda:

- Discussions on improvements in skills. As a guideline, the unskilled play as defined in the Introduction of this book can be used.

- Discussions on the abilities of the coaches to reinforce training curricula in games.

- Airing complaints regarding referees, players' time in games, unfair team selections of players (at the start of the season), parents' observations, and so on.

To meet these objectives, some specifics should be addressed. They are the following:

False praise is frequently given by poorly skilled coaches. Experienced individuals frequently see coaches complimenting certain players for purely aggressive play or unproductive tactics during actual games. Experienced individuals should be sought to voice their opinions at meetings held to discuss both skillful and unskillful play. If all play is skillful, the point is moot, but there will probably be some negative activities reported.

An example of a counter-productive comment would be a coach's yelling out "good try" for a flamboyant but unskilled activity. This activity could be, for an aggressive but semi-skilled player, taking an extremely hard kick at a fast loose-ball with a once-on long kick, or making a small-angled kick at the goal. This is certainly a mistake when this same player could have settled the ball and passed it to an unguarded onside teammate near the goal.

False compliments can be disturbing or confusing to players who are learning. They can be especially harmful to slower learning players who are earnestly trying to apply new skills correctly. Praise for incorrect activities is counter-productive as it does not reflect sound soccer techniques. Players that earnestly apply their training could eventually be the real stars of the future, but only if rewards go to those who are performing or endeavoring to play skillfully (rewards, in this instance, mean honest compliments along with more time spent in games); often, however, players are chastised for making mistakes and then pay the price by having very little game time. It should also be pointed out that unskillful yet aggressive individuals usually finish their soccer careers by the time that they are about 16.

House leagues should refrain from awarding trophies. These leagues should generally be the training teams that support the traveling leagues (if they co-exist). Even if there are no traveling teams, it is still a good idea not to award trophies to special players or house league teams. Trophies lead to a premature competitiveness. Premature competitiveness tends to militate against the players' initiatives for learning required skills at their own pace. Not awarding trophies to young house league players is an example of your town's league's responsibility for the overall development of all young soccer players.

Victory salutes by a goal scoring player should not be condoned. They can make it seem that the team contributed little to assist in the goal. This could have an adverse effect on the morale of the team.

In summary, a healthy organization is one where all players get fair treatment and are encouraged to practice what they are taught.

As mentioned in the Introduction, each league should have a charter. It could be as simple as: "The objective of this club is to promote fairness to all and to attain the highest level of soccer possible by using any fair means to obtain this objective."

The objective would then be obtained by installing club rules for all to abide by, along with a process to amend these rules from time to time. These rules (separate from the charter) should include activities such as training methods and objectives, a player's allotted time in a game, refereeing objectives, and the requirements of each and every officer (coaches are included here). Enforcement of the rules and sanctions for infractions are an absolute necessity.

With everything else in place as discussed above, there should then be an agenda for teaching playing skills. It must also be reinforced, if one is to expect the necessary skills to take hold. This agenda should be applied to entry level players or when remedial improvement is needed for any team or league lacking in basic skills. This is the subject and objective of this book. These skills in general are as follows:

- Trapping the soccer ball dead at the feet (all team players are included—even the goalkeeper, but not as extensively). As soon as this is realized, shielding is to be introduced and blended with trapping the ball dead at the feet.

- Retaining possession of the ball.

- Employing a strong defense. Defending must be the primary goal of all 11 soccer positions.

- When, and only when, the first three items are solidly in place should some emphasis be placed on scoring goals by the forward-moving players. But scoring goals should never become the overall objective. Rather, skillful team power is a better objective.

The question might naturally arise as to how will goals be scored if offensive goal scoring methods are not part of the early schedule of learning? The answer is that one need not be concerned as it is only natural for soccer players to practice scoring on their own, even if it is done incorrectly. Some things must come first, or they will likely never come. Therefore, one need not be concerned with the lack of early training of offensive methods, because goals will occur anyway.

On Trapping, Shielding and Aggression

The mark of an excellent soccer player is the ability to trap a soccer ball dead at his or her feet. This takes self-discipline. Trapping a ball dead at the feet while under pressure from an opponent is extremely difficult if it is not done while employing the technique called shielding to maintain the ball's possession. Unskilled and untrained players without this skill cannot or will not trap the ball when an opponent is bearing down on them.

It is essential to trap a ball nearly all of the time. When trapping in conjunction with shielding is performed, maintaining possession of the trapped ball is a likely outcome, provided that the trapping player does not get intimidated by the opponent. Furthermore, subsequent shielding of the ball ensures that a player can continue to maintain possession.

Trapping and shielding are two distinct techniques. They must be learned separately before they can be merged into the *ball-possessive* trap. So the order of learning this combined technique is to first master the trap. Once trapping has become second nature, shielding is to be added.

Here is an example of how trapping correctly builds strong players. My two youngest sons were generally mid-field players, but at times they also played forward and were top scorers. Since they were about seven or eight years of age, they had been taught to trap the ball dead at their feet and to shield it. They were superb at this because I demanded it. One year, the older of the two boys was selected to play center half back for an under 18 year old team in a tournament. He was only 14 at the time and clearly smaller in stature than the older players on both teams.

This was one of his best games because every ball that came to him either high, low, fast or slow was trapped dead at his feet. He would then dribble the ball a short distance before passing it on the ground to one of the older and stronger teammates—that is, he settled the ball for them in order that they could play the game with maximum ball control. Even though he was apprehensive about dribbling the ball against his more powerful opponents, he had clearly shown all players on both teams how a true ball control game can be played, even by amateurs. My youngest son was also very skillful at trapping and shielding the ball. He was always chosen to play on the State Select Team because of these abilities.

Note that a good player can make traps of many types regardless of how the ball arrives. All traps (except one, the Body Trap covered in Chapter 4) bring the ball down in front of the player's feet. Other trapping methods are covered in later drills, but the most commonly used trap, the Inside-of-the-Foot Trap for Ground Balls will be taught as the principle one. As skills develop, other traps can be learned. After these traps have been practiced, learning to protect the ball will follow in the drills.

Learning to protect the ball (shielding) is an important area for the development of soccer players and is a major topic in this book. This aspect of the training will contribute to winning games. When training is mostly concentrated on scoring goals, it is centered around the forward players and some mid-fielders, and means that approximately half of the team is not considered in the overall equation. But with skillful training in areas such as short passes, trapping and shielding, longer periods of ball possession will be achieved. Your team will be on offense longer and thus will have a greater possibility for scoring. When a longer period of offense occurs in the mid-field and in front of the opponent's goal, the overall effect can be to disorient your opponent's defense.

Every soccer coach naturally desires to have 11 players on the field who are in top physical condition, are fast and have the utmost skills. In reality, there are usually about two or three excellent players, several reasonably good ones and a few poor. The coach must work around the problems that occur with the less strong players. Even skillful players in highly competitive situations can become weak in the face of an aggressive opposition.

Can this problem be resolved in that the weaker players become stronger? To some extent, yes. But first, it should be pointed out that there are many players who have the correct amount of "legal" aggression because they have been playing this way all of their lives. There are also those players that have joined soccer for recreation and are not normally aggressive for whatever reason. How then can less aggressive children play to their maximum potential? The question becomes answered when the players are taught the correct amount of aggressive behavior (soccer-legal aggression) through a certain drill.

On Competitiveness and Balanced Aggression

Aggressive activity is a necessary part of this sport. Sometimes it is not sufficient, and other times it is overdone, but a balanced and accepted amount of aggression should be the goal. For your players to compete at all levels in the game, it is necessary that they play at the acceptable aggression level of their league. North American youth soccer is composed of boys and girls playing on mixed teams, as well as girls playing on all-girls teams, and boys on all-boys teams.

Some skillful players lack the proper aggression and are at a great disadvantage. For instance, while a timid player is trying to trap a ball (and properly shield it), with an overly aggressive yet unskillful opponent bearing down on him, he is most likely overly preoccupied with this player and is not concentrating on executing his move properly. Consequently, the trapping player will probably lose the ball to the less skillful opponent. Therefore the discussion of proper aggression becomes a co-requirement to be placed alongside of the strived for skill level promoted throughout this book. Most young players can benefit from this knowledge and training, but not all players wish to upgrade their level of aggression.

The following is an example of a player who did not wish to move up the aggressive ladder and is a story that I have often told. Kristen was a 12 year old wing fullback on our team. On offense, she would trap the ball and dribble it a few feet, then pass it off. She did this well and usually made fewer errors than her male counterparts. She was helpful on offense, but could have contributed more if she was more aggressive. Her strength was in her defense. She was not a versatile player, but was a strong asset to our team's defense. She was taught to back up with an attacker and not attempt to tackle the ball unless the dribbler clearly had lost control of it.

She was exceptional at defense. She had perfected this most important defensive move and few players ever got by her. In many situations, she would end up with the ball because young dribbling players eventually lose the ball's control. She had the self-discipline to back up with any attacking player and not obey any impulse or external pressure to try to gain possession of the ball unless the dribbler had lost just the slightest control of it. If the player did not lose control of the ball, she would stand her ground flawlessly, as she had been trained to do, and not attempt the tackle — this is also extremely important to defense.

One particular incident occurred during a Sunday afternoon game and is a colorful example of her skill. She was in her wing defensive position and backing up with a dribbling opponent named Bobby. He was endeavoring to pass her. His mother happened to be nearby and seated just off the side line. As Kristen was backing up, Bobby's mother shouted several times to her son, "Don't be afraid of her, Bobby." Kristen remained calm as she backed up with him. Maintaining her usual cool and confident self, she stayed with him as he advanced down field. Within about thirty seconds of the first shouts from the boy's mother, Bobby made his mistake, the one that Kristen was waiting for. She ended up with the ball, much to the embarrassment of Bobby and his mother. The mechanics of her movements were predictable, precise and reliable. The only problem with Kristen was that she did not go beyond her capacity to aid in attacks. She was not interested in going beyond her present level.

The point of this story is that Kristen could have been a potentially superb soccer player because she was as smart as she was coachable. She followed instructions and learned what was being taught. What she didn't possess was the desire to be more aggressive. She was exposed to the drill to teach legal soccer aggression, but she still chose to remain nonaggressive instead of being a more rounded player. One should be realistic and understand that this sport is not for everyone and especially not for those who do not come up to the proper aggressive level, whether male or female.

The following example shows aggressiveness training that was fruitful. While in Park Ridge, one of the younger coed teams had gone halfway through the season and had not won a single game. The coach came to me and complained that several of the players were missing practices and not showing up for the games. I then decided to hold the practices myself for two weeks and show the coach what was required, and also to teach the players proper aggression with the Shoulder Charge Drill. The results of the aggressive drill were very positive. This team won two out of their last four games and the players and coach were as elated as if they had started off the season and finished it undefeated.

Over the years, I had found the above example to be the norm, not the exception for this kind of conditioning. Naturally, caution must be considered.

Soccer athletes can be very competitive and they can be very aggressive, sometimes too aggressive, and noncontact soccer can become a contact sport, even though contact is "illegal" in almost all instances. The objective is to promote a balanced aggression that is within the legal limits of the Laws of the Game; and this usually occurs. I have found, however, that only those who wish to be more aggressive will benefit from the proper training.

When the two genders come together in a highly competitive sport such as soccer, girls are often intimidated by the roughness that boys are accustomed to. Therefore, they are at a disadvantage as portrayed in this hypothetical example: A loose ball is being aggressively charged by a boy and a girl from opposite teams (neither having been trained in the proper soccer aggression). Both players are racing at the ball to gain its possession. If one of the two individuals hesitates in the slightest, it will most likely be won by the more aggressive person. In most cases, everything else being equal, the boy will win out. However, with the proper training and desire, both players have an equal chance of obtaining possession.

On Defense

Against a worthy opponent, defense is the most important ingredient in winning soccer. In my early years coaching and managing teams, my players received training in ball control skills and it had reasonably positive effects on them. Nonetheless, winning championships was a slow, uphill battle because I was following the practices of the more experienced coaches. Even though the players were rigorously trained with all sorts of drills, there was still something lacking. After pondering for years, I uncovered the flaw in my approach: Like so many coaches all around me, I was spending nearly all of my coaching time on the development of offensive measures. The problem of producing stronger winning teams, I learned, had its roots in defense.

For about ten years I had been intensively involved with every type of activity related to youth and adult soccer, especially coaching. I had seen so many situations that were a prelude to a goal that I began to foresee a goal scored a few seconds before it happened: It was the same situation over and over. It became evident that the main cause for losing games was rooted in the defensive players and defense in general.

The formation of the defensive players seems often to break down just before a goal is scored or nearly scored. At this moment, defensive players go scrambling in disarray. On the other hand, when an attack buildup is thwarted, the defensive players as well as the mid-fielders are usually in their normal positions. This observation was the key to winning championships. The secret has always been known to some, but I had to learn just how to apply and maintain sound defensive techniques. The reasoning was so solid that after applying defensive strategies, I learned that the offensive players were more focused on their scoring objective because they were not hampered by the sloppy defensive play of their own team.

The following is an example of a single player's defensive technique, I have chosen a story about a boy named Richard that I coached when he was between eight and 12. Richard was on the small side and a winger defense man for our team. He was attentive and alert and, most of all, coachable. He was taught "never to attack the ball" on defense. He was taught to back up with a dribbling opponent and not make any moves towards the ball unless the opponent lost the slightest bit of control. Richard was superb at this, as he was mentally keen and dependable. He was one of the best defense players that I had ever coached, because he would often dribble the ball before passing it off to another player in a better offensive position than himself. He preferred the defensive wing and never faulted on his backing up technique. Richard held the key for maintaining a solid defense, as very few goals were scored by opposing teams on his wing side.

At the age of 13, he went to another team for a year. I saw him play in a game at the end of that season and was surprised that he had played so poorly. In defense, he was now attacking the ball and being beaten by attacking players. I surmised that his present coach over-rode my teachings and taught him that the defense person is supposed to tackle the ball from the attacking players: This is common with most novice soccer coaches and, because of this, Richard had lost his edge.

The next season he returned to our team but with a weak approach to defense. Initially, he was making defensive errors that he never had made previously on our team. Goals were being scored by opposing teams very frequently on his wing. With much coaching, it took to the second half of the season for him to come back to his old self, to once again prevent goals from being scored on his wing. Fortunately he regained his superb technical defensive skill, but had he not come back to our team, I doubt that he would have. This example also illustrates the importance of requiring coaches to employ identical training methods (as well as to stress defensive abilities).

The message is two-fold:

- Defensive strategy must be maintained for dependability and not be undersold in soccer strategy. Richard, confused by his new coach, naturally had to follow orders because he was the coachable type. He followed the instructions of a coach who did not know the basics—that a defense person must never attack the ball unless it is out of the control of the dribbler.

- The progress of players who are taught different methods by different coaches can, and often will, be impeded. This is why it is so important to have all players in a league learn *the correct techniques* that are reinforced by all coaches.

These techniques (defensive) can be classified into four categories.

- Shielding (it is difficult to classify this technique: It is clearly defensive, except that the player shielding the ball is really on the offensive).

- Backing up with an opponent.

- Covering an opponent when the opponents are in possession of the ball; sometimes called man to man defense.

- Giving responsibility for control of the defense to the goalkeeper.

The Overall View of This Book

To round out a good soccer player, he or she must be drilled in proper and acceptable aggression, trapping and shielding, and defensive techniques. With these techniques mastered, the player is ready to learn offensive techniques through drills that present realistic game situations.

The four defensive categories are covered in the various chapters, along with offensive tactics; the mastery of skillful techniques alone cannot, however, make great athletes. Proper aggressive behavior is also a requirement, but not the type of excessively aggressive and often violent behavior that is frequently substituted for a lack of skill, often going beyond legal tactics.

For a player to be competitive in soccer, he or she must want the ball. This means that an excellent soccer player cannot be intimidated by other players on the opposing team or even by teammates, so his skillful activities must be balanced with permissible aggressiveness. This is why it is important for all soccer players to be properly instructed in this area.

Choosing the drills for your practices should be determined by the skill level of your team. If you are uncertain which level most of your team members have achieved, it is recommended that you start at the lowest level and work upwards. If you are in a position to regulate the training of your league, then it should be considered a mandate to prescribe league requirements for the managers and coaches to follow. In addition, if your league does subscribe to the idea of uniform training for your team managers and coaches to follow, it would be necessary to require that they attend two or three instructional classes prior to the season's training commencement.

The Overall View on Drills

There are some general rules discussed below that ordinarily apply to all drills in addition to the information shown in the drill figures. Adherence to these rules should give a coach maximum control over the drill as well as the soccer players.

- Players should not be distributed too far over the training field. Unsupervised players too far from the coach's view and control tend to lose sight of the drill objective.

- Players are to remain within their field as set out by field markers. As the exercises progress and the players move around, they would tend to lose perspective as to how far they should be spaced from each other if field markers are not used. Mark off the distance for each player with any convenient but safe type of field marker such as a cone, jersey, ball, water container, etc. **Do not use any type of field marker that is pointed or hazardous in any manner**.

- Players should not be crisscrossing onto others' playing fields. Field marked locations, illustrated in drill diagrams, will minimize this problem.

- Each player should bring the following to practices and games: (1) warm clothing and rain gear (if applicable); (2) a personal container of drinking water; (3) their own ball—at practices only.

- In drills where players pair off and there is an odd number of players, form one or more groups of three.

- During practices, if any exercise is not taken seriously or is not understood, recall all players and give a repeat demonstration. Do this as often as necessary.

- Always allow the players to perform their drills at their own pace. Pressure imposed upon them for speed learning will invariably sacrifice the accuracy needed for precision.

- A plan should be made in preparation for each practice. Outline the time required for each segment. For example:

  Warmups, 10 minutes.

  Running, 10 minutes.

  Break, 5 minutes.

  Lecture, demonstration and first drill, 15 minutes.

  Lecture, demonstration and second drill, 15 minutes.

  Lecture, demonstration and third drill, 15 minutes.

  Short scrimmage games, 15 minutes.

  Full scrimmage game, 35 minutes.

- **All players should be medically fit and properly warmed up with stretching exercises and running prior to the commencement of the drills. The appropriate fitness and conditioning should be overseen by health and medical professionals.**

2a. Basic Field Drills— Offensive

Drill 2.1

THE INSTEP KICK

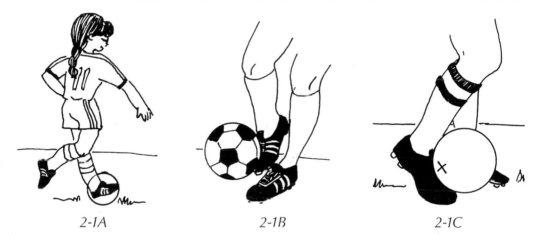

| 2-1A | 2-1B | 2-1C |

Illustration 2-1. The Basic Instep Kick and the Angled Instep Kick. *Illustration 2-1A* shows a player in proper position for the kick. *Illustration 2-1B* shows the Basic Instep Kick with the ball being struck with the laces. *Illustration 2-1C* shows the contact point between the ball and the foot at the side of the laces for the Angled Instep Kick.

The Mechanics

The Instep Kick shown in *Illustration 2-1A* is one of the most common kicks used in soccer. There are two variations of this kick based upon the size of the foot. The fundamental version, called the Basic Instep Kick, is shown in *Illustration 2-1B*. With the basic version of this kick, the ball is contacted with the center of the kicking foot laces. This kick is used with small feet. When the size of the foot is greater than size eight the other version, the Angled Instep Kick, is utilized. In this case the kicking foot is angled such that when kicking, the toe does not inadvertently contact the ground during the kick. The Angled Instep Kick is shown in *Illustration 2-1C* (see previous page) where the laces are contacted off to the side.

As shown in the illustrations, the nonkicking foot is placed along side of the ball with the toes of this foot located at its front: This is not a natural action and a conscious effort must be made to place the nonkicking foot towards the front of the ball. If it is desired to place the ball in the air, then the toe of the nonkicking foot is not placed as far forward.

To produce a good kick, the head must be kept down with the eyes fixed on the ball during the entire kicking process. It is necessary to follow through the kick to obtain both power and accuracy. The kicking foot should follow a straight line during the kick and the leg should not follow an arched curve or accuracy will often be sacrificed. When the Angled Instep Kick is utilized, the ball is not kicked at its center; it is kicked slightly offcenter and this offcenter impact causes it to spin. As a result of the spin, the ball will curve in the direction of the spin.

> *Note 1:* With the Basic Instep Kick, the ball is hit in its center and no spin will result. With a right-footed Angled Instep Kick however, the ball will curve to the left while a left-footed kick will cause the ball to curve to the right. To attain accuracy, the player must compensate for the spin.

> *Note 2:* When using this kick for scoring outdoors, it is more effective to place the ball to the lower corner. For indoor soccer, a high kick to the upper corner of the goal is more effective.

This drill has two parts, the Static Drill and the Dynamic Drill. The static or stationary ball version of the drill requires that the player kick the ball without taking the normal running start. The dynamic version requires that the player dribble and kick the ball while moving. Both drills are set up as a contest to keep young players interested.

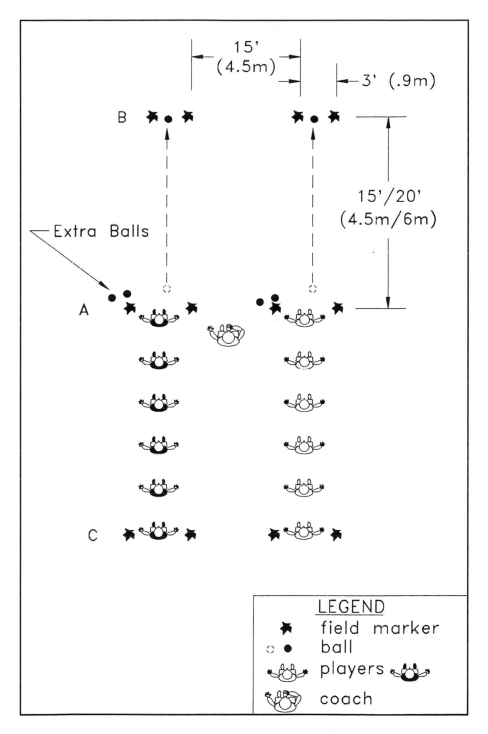

15'
(4.5m)

3' (.9m)

B

Extra Balls

A

15'/20'
(4.5m/6m)

C

LEGEND
★ field marker
◌ ● ball
players
coach

Figure 2-1. The Kicking Drill

The Drills

Version 1 (Static Situation)

- Set up the drill as shown in *Figure 2-1* (see previous page). The distance from A to B can be adjusted according to the players' ages and abilities. The players line up in two columns located at A.

- Both columns will be competing to see which team can score the most goals. Balance both columns with players of about equal athletic abilities. The first players of each team are to remain between their field markers during the kick. Note that Location C is not used for this stage of the drill.

- For the static drill version, the player is to kick a stationary ball through the goal by applying the kicking procedure outlined above. The contest rules are as follows: (1) The contest requires that each kicking player refrain from looking up after the ball is kicked; (2) The player may only look up after the ball passes the goal; this is very important and is necessary for accuracy. This is to instill in the young player that keeping her eyes on the ball is essential and that looking up during the kick can only make the kick more inaccurate. Not following this rule will disallow a scored goal; (3) Each player gets three kicks. (One average-scoring player is to be picked to kick by taking another turn, if the other team contains an extra player); (4) The teams are to keep score of the number of goals scored; (5) The teams do their kicking in alternation to allow the coach to monitor each player's motions during each kick; (6) After each player gets her turn, she is to retrieve the balls.

- Naturally, the team with the most goals wins. It should be noted that players should learn at their own pace and that competition for speed amongst teammates is not always wise. Speed of application for a skill can cause a player to get careless for fear of going too slow. For this drill or any drill, the correct procedure should take precedent over speed.

- **The coach should observe the placement of the nonkicking foot at the front of the ball and assure that the kickers are keeping eyes on the ball during the entire kick.**

Version 2 (Dynamic Situation)

- During this drill, players make their kicks at the goal while dribbling the ball. It is more practical than the previous drill, but should only be substituted for static kick drill when the players are performing the static shooting in a satisfactory manner; and after having been exposed to dribbling drills. (The kick used in either of these drills is not the ultimate instep kick for scoring goals: There is yet another version. It is called The Under-the-Body-Instep Kick and is covered in Chapter 5: This version is preferred when an opponent is near.)

- For this drill, place a set of four field markers at location C, 10' (3 m) behind the field markers located at A.

- All players will now stand behind the field markers located at C instead of at location A.

- Each player is to dribble the ball to the field markers located at A and then take a shot at the goal. The requirements of this drill are as follows: (1) As above, the players cannot look up until the shot has reached at the goal. If a player looks up prematurely, the shot is disqualified; (2) The ball is to be dribbled near the feet.

- For this version, the player is to kick the ball through the goal by applying the kicking procedure outlined above. The contest rules are the same as above and repeated: (1) The contest requires that each kicking player refrain from looking up after the ball is kicked; (2) The player may only look up after the ball passes the goal; this is very important and is necessary for accuracy. This is to instill in the young player that keeping her eyes on the ball is essential and that looking up during the kick can only make the kick more inaccurate. Not following this rule will disallow a scored goal; (3) Each player gets three kicks during her turn; (4) The teams are to keep score of the number of goals scored; (5) The teams do their kicking in alternation to allow the coach to monitor each player's motions during each kick; (6) After each player gets her turn, she is to retrieve the balls.

- The team with the most goals wins.

- **The coach should be looking to insure that the ball is dribbled near the feet prior to the kick. He should also be observing that the kickers are keeping their eyes on the ball during the entire kick and that the nonkicking foot is located at the front of the ball.**

Drill 2.2

THE LOW INSIDE-OF-THE-FOOT
TRAP FOR GROUND BALLS

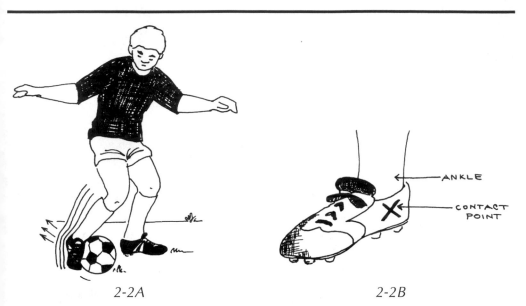

2-2A   2-2B

Illustration 2-2. The Low Inside-of-the-Foot Trap for Ground Balls. The shock absorbing motion of the foot is shown in *Illustration 2-2A* and the contact point on the foot is shown in *Illustration 2-2B*.

The Mechanics

This technique is generally used for trapping ground balls (rolling balls), but it is also used when an air ball arrives at or very near the ground of a trapping player's foot. It is contacted with the inside of the foot. *Illustration 2-2* shows the Low Inside-of-the-Foot Trap.

The Low Inside-of-the-Foot Trap is made with the ball contacting that part of the foot just below the ankle and on the soft part at the top of the arch. The ball must meet this correct spot on the foot to stop the ball dead (the ball can roll a few inches, but it must not be out of reach of the trapper). The trap is correctly made when the foot is allowed to recoil at the moment of contact with the ball. The ball must not rise after the trap, but fall. If the ball rises, the foot has contacted the ball below its parallel reference plane (this reference plane is the ball's equator that is parallel to the ground). If the trapping foot is too high, the ball will pass under the foot. Only if the ball drops down and stops in front of the trapping foot can the player then make his next move without the necessity of chasing after the ball. This is the optimum trap; and anything less causes an excessive amount of time for the ball to be settled, thus risking its loss to an opponent.

As the players anticipate receiving the ball they must develop the habit of going to it and stopping just before the trap is made. Players that wait for the ball to come to them find out that very often someone else beats them to it. It is advisable that the coach point out to players not familiar with good trapping techniques that they are to go to the ball, then stop before making contact with it. It must be noted that very few players can trap a ball dead while they are moving and so this idea should be made clear to all players.

Players must habitually learn to keep their eyes on the ball during trapping, but immediately after the trap, they are to look up and around the field. These two eye movements are vital for helping players concentrate on making the trap and their next move correctly.

To complete this exercise, the ball should be dribbled a few times after performing a correct trap. This is to teach players that they are never to stand still after making a trap while deciding upon their next move.

The Drill

- Set up the drill as shown in *Figure 2-2* (see page 26). The teammates will be 15' to 20' (4.5 m to 6 m) apart, depending on their age or abilities. For this discussion we have five sets of players arranged in five columns. Each pair of players shares a ball for the purpose of kicking it back and forth to each other (an odd numbered player will form into a threesome). The drill is performed in the following manner with the focus on players #1 and #2 referenced in *Figure 2-2*.

Stage 1

- With each pair of players positioned as shown in the figure, *Player #1* kicks the ball to *Player #2* with sufficient velocity to duplicate a pass in a game.

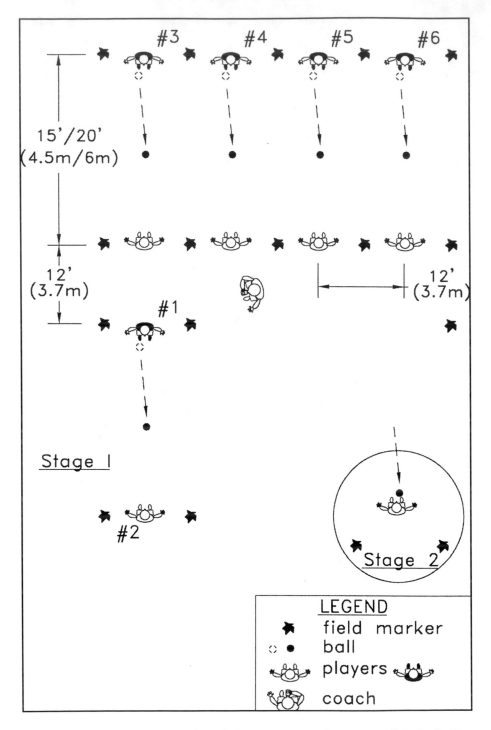

Figure 2-2. The Low Inside-of-the-Foot Trap for Ground Balls Drill

Text within the figure:

#3   #4   #5   #6

15'/20'
(4.5m/6m)

12'
(3.7m)

12'
(3.7m)

#1

Stage 1

#2

Stage 2

LEGEND
★ field marker
◌ ● ball
players
coach

Stage 2

- *Player #2* goes to the ball (this is imperative as stated earlier, in game situations a player cannot wait for the ball to come to him). Before the trap is made, *Player #2* must stop.

- As this player receives the ball, he is to trap the ball with the instep of the foot such that it stops in front of the trapping foot. The trapped ball of each player must travel downward, not upwards and the player must watch the ball during the entire trapping process.

- After the ball is trapped, it is to be dribbled back to a field marker. This playing the ball with the feet (dribbling) after the trap is necessary to simulate a game situation: The ball must immediately be moved away from the trapping location after it is under control of the trapper. The player then turns around and kicks the ball back to the partner who duplicates the moves as just described. *Note:* The player will be making a blind turn here. In a game situation, he can easily lose the ball to an opponent this way; however, in Chapter 5, the proper turning method will be shown through the drill, Turning While Dribbling.

- Run the exercise for about five minutes then rotate the players in each pair group enabling each player to change partners: i.e., *Player #3* goes to position #4, *Player #4* goes to position #5, *Player #5* goes to position #6 and *Player #6* goes to position #3, etc. Repeat this drill two more times with rotated players. The total time for the exercise should be approximately 15 minutes.

- *Note:* the players must take this somewhat repetitive and tedious exercise seriously. They must have the realization, by an adequate explanation, that it is the first step for more advanced trapping techniques.

- **The coach should be observing that the trappers keep their eyes on the ball during trapping, that the ball does not rise just after impact and that the ball stops just in front of the feet.**

Drill 2.3
THE CHEST TRAP

The Mechanics

This Chest Trap is used for trapping balls arriving in the air or balls that bounce up to chest height from the ground. See *Illustration 2-3A* for

2-3A   2-3B

Illustration 2-3. The Chest Trap. *Illustration 2-3A* shows a typical chest trap for a male. *Illustration 2-3B* shows a typical chest trap for a female. Females may protect themselves by crossing their arms as shown. The area just below the wrist, as shown (with the arm angled upwards), is the preferred contact area.

the chest trapping technique. The Chest Trap is made differently with males and females. For males, it is made with the ball contacting the chest just above the sternum. Females are permitted to cross their arms and place them in front of their chest as shown in *Illustration 2-3B*.

Very often, a player can choose between trapping the ball with the chest or to head pass it to another player. The head pass is useful for the correct situations and is often the easier choice to make because it does not require controlling the ball to the same extent as the Chest Trap. For ball control soccer, it is almost always advantageous to the team for a player to get control of the ball. With this in mind, the Chest Trap should be the preferred choice on the field for most occasions.

The rules of this trap are as follows:

- It is important to keep one's eyes on the ball during the entire procedure.
- The player is to go to the ball, i.e., not wait for the ball to come to him.

- As the flight path becomes clear to the player, he is to align himself with the path of the ball and angle the body so as to contact the chest (or forearm for females) in a perpendicular fashion.

- Just before contact, the player is to stop.

- If the ball is arriving from the air, the upper body should be bent backwards depending upon the angle of flight of the ball. If the ball is arriving at the player from the ground on a bounce, the upper body will be bent forward. In both cases it is desired that the ball contact a perpendicular surface of the body to keep the ball from bouncing in some nonpreferred direction.

- As the ball and the player come into contact, the player is to recoil (withdraw the chest or chest and arms) to reduce the ball's speed upon impact.

- It is preferred that the ball initially drop downwards after contact with the body; however, on sharply inclined trajectories the chest becomes angled with only a few degrees from the horizontal, causing the ball to rise slightly after body contact. *Note:* The smaller the chest angle with the vertical, the quicker the ball will drop to the ground (provided that the ball initially falls and does not rise immediately after contact with the chest).

- As soon as the ball has dropped to the ground, the player must get control of it and immediately dribble it off in any direction.

The Drill

Set up the drill as shown in *Figure 2-3* (see page 30). The players will be 10' to 15' (3–4.5 m) from the coach, depending on their age or abilities. They are also placed at a 20–30 degree angle from the direction of the flight of the ball. There are two versions of this drill: Version 1 requires that the ball arrives at the player from the air and Version 2 requires that the ball arrives at the player from the ground.

Version 1 (The ball arriving from the air)

- The coach is to throw the ball underhanded using both hands to the first player in line. The ball is thrown to peak at an altitude of about 6' or 8' (1.8 m to 2.4 m) above the ground midway between the coach and the trapping player. After the ball is thrown and in

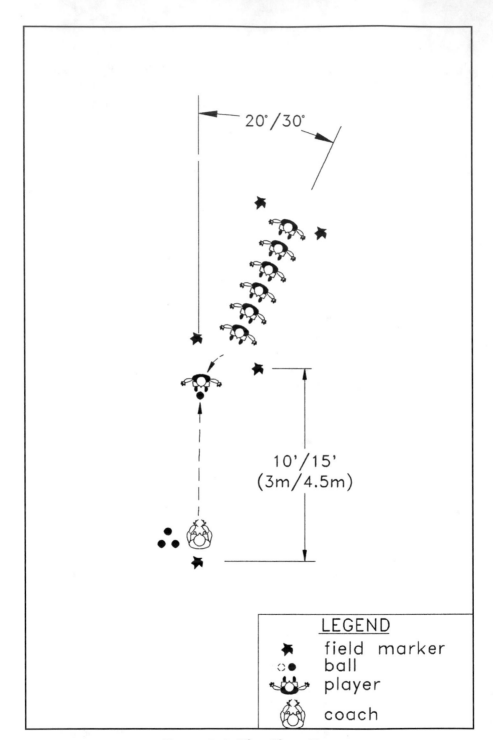

20°/30°

10'/15'
(3m/4.5m)

LEGEND
★ field marker
○● ball
🧍 player
👤 coach

Figure 2-3. The Chest Trap

flight, the player is to align himself with the oncoming direction of the ball (inline with the coach and the path of the ball) and trap it according to the method described above.

- As the ball is trapped, it should not rise above the horizontal after impact with the chest. If it bounces excessively high or to the side of the player, it has not been performed correctly.

- After the ball drops to the ground, the player is to get the ball under the control of the feet and dribble it back to the coach.

- Each player should make three good traps. If the ball is thrown poorly, the throw is to be repeated. After completing three good traps, the player is to return to the end of the line to have two more turns at chest trapping.

- **The coach should observe that the body is aligned with the ball trajectory during the trap. Also observe that the ball does not rise greatly upon chest impact (or arm impact for females) and that the eyes are kept on the ball during the trap.**

Version 2 (The ball bouncing from the ground)

- The coach is to bounce the ball by throwing it overhand with one or both hands to the ground permitting it to bounce up to chest height of the trapper.

- The trapping procedure is then performed in a similar fashion as in *Version 1*, but with the trapper leaning with his chest downward to keep the ball from rising.

- Each player should make a total of three good traps as stated above. Repeat this drill two more times. Note: If time is short, this portion of the drill should be run during the successive soccer practice.

- **The coach should observe that the body is in line with the trajectory of the ball. Also, observe that the ball does not rise upon chest impact (or arm impact for females) and that the player's eyes are on the ball during the trap.**

Drill 2.4
BASIC DRIBBLING

The Mechanics

Dribbling a ball is performed by pushing it with the feet, the ball is not tapped. The pushing action with every step allows a player more control over the ball. When dribbling the ball near opponents, players should slow down to a point where they can be certain to maintain control of the ball that is to remain near the feet. It may be pushed a little further out ahead of the dribbling player if no opponents are around, but it must still remain close enough to a player so he can retain its control. It must be emphasized that the ball should be dribbled near the feet whenever possible. When dribbling, the ball is pushed with the inside of the foot or the outside of the foot. The ball can generally be contacted on the foot well in front of the ankle, back more towards the ankle, or the top of the three smaller toes; however, it may at times also come into contact with just about any part of the foot. The points of contact can continuously change at any time during the dribble, but, when dribbling up to an opponent that one wishes to fake and pass, dribbling using the outside of only one foot is recommended.

Players must also learn to dribble the ball without looking at it. It is important that players learn to watch the field for opportunities and opponents. But when near opponents, the dribbling player must look at the ball and keep it as near as possible to the feet. It is important to distinguish here that during other maneuvers players must look at the ball, such as when shielding, kicking, heading and trapping.

The Drill

- This is another drill performed as a contest for young players to hold their interest. It is a kind of relay race. Set up the field as shown in *Figure 2-4.* Balance the teams with players of equal abilities. Have the players on each team stand behind field markers located at A.

- At the start of the drill, the first player in both lines is to have a ball and dribble it through the field markers at Location B and towards the right side of the field marker located at C. *Note 1:* This is a race. It is most important that each player dribble the ball as near to the feet as possible to make a smooth passing around the

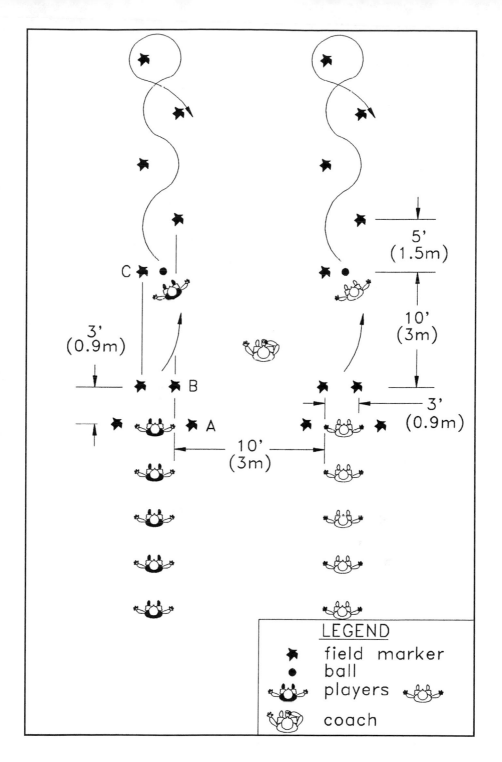

Figure 2-4. The Basic Dribbling Drill

Illustration 2-4.
Basic Shielding
While Dribbling

field markers; however, dribbling correctly is still encouraged. *Note 2:* As with other drills throughout this book, accuracy and care take precedence over speed.

- The player is to continue to dribble the ball through the field markers and around the last one located at C, then pass back through the field markers located at B. If the dribbler does not go around each field marker, he is to return and do so.

- After the player has returned to location B, he is to pass the ball to the waiting teammate located at A.

- This next player is then to continue with the relay until all players have had one turn. If there is an odd number of players, one average skilled player is to have another turn on the opposing team. This completes the relay.

- Repeat this drill two more times.

- **The coach should determine that each player dribbles the ball near the feet even though this will generally slow the player down. It will, however, ensure that the players do not dribble too far beyond the field markers. The players are to be encouraged not to look at the ball while dribbling.**

Drill 2.5
Basic Shielding While Dribbling

The Mechanics

Basic Shielding While Dribbling is shown in *Illustration 2-4*. The terms shielding and screening will be used interchangeably. This soccer skill enables a player to maintain ball possession when in close proximity to an opponent. It also assumes that the player has possession of the ball and is

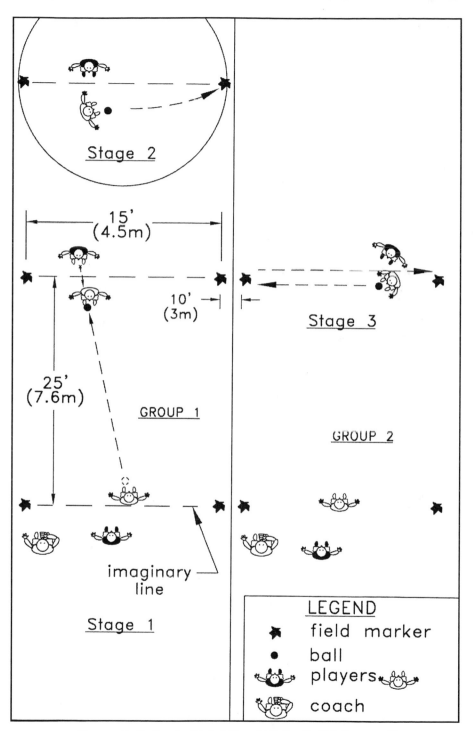

Stage 2

15'
(4.5m)

10'
(3m)

Stage 3

25'
(7.6m)

GROUP 1

GROUP 2

imaginary
line

Stage 1

LEGEND

★ field marker
● ball
players
coach

Figure 2-5. Basic Shielding While Dribbling Drill

dribbling it when a nearby opponent is endeavoring to remove the ball from this dribbling player. Players must master this technique in order to become proficient and confident in dribbling. Without this skill, players will soon become ineffective; its importance cannot be stressed enough. Shielding immediately after the trap will be covered in a later drill.

Shielding the soccer ball has many uses and this drill emphasizes the use of one's body to screen the ball from an opponent while dribbling. Shielding the ball from an opponent is performed by orienting one's body such that it is always between the opponent and the ball. It can also be used to screen the ball from two opponents as long as the dribbling player keeps both opponents in sight and maintains a position between these players and the ball.

Illustration 2-4 shows a player shielding the ball from an opponent. The player's arms may be initially up to gain her balance, but they must not be used to keep the other player from the ball; the body does that. The dribbling player is arched backwards to further keep the ball from the reach of the opponent. Often there is contact here, but as long as the player dribbling the ball does not do body pushing into the opponent, the play is legal. (It is not legal for the opponent to make contact either.)

In order for this move to be constantly effective, the dribbler must push the ball in a direction that keeps it out of reach from the opponent. Doing so, she must not only keep her eye on the ball, but also keep her eyes on the opponent by peripheral vision or by watching his shadows. The dribbling player must also steer herself in some direction and not remain in the same area of the field. Generally, this player will be looking for an open player to pass the ball to, so she must also be observing other action on the field. During this drill the players are constrained to dribble along an imaginary line.

The Drill

- Set up the drill as shown in *Figure 2-5*. This figure shows two groups of players with field markers spaced 15' (4.5 m) apart. Players in similar jerseys are on the same team. There will be as many groups of players as can be made from the available people. For this discussion, we will only be initially concerned with the Group 1 players; containing four members. The field markers separate the participants by 25' (7.6 m), depending upon their age and abilities. Field markers connected by the dashed lines signify an imaginary line that constrains the players. The players may only move along this imaginary line. However, when the player is to trap the ball from a teammate's pass, she is to go to the ball and dribble it back to the line and thus must come off the line for this phase of the drill: This instills into the players that they must always go to the ball for the trap.

Illustration 2-5.
The Push-Pass Kick

- The first player of Group 1 passes the ball to his teammate as shown in **Stage 1**. After making the trap, the dribbling player is to dribble the ball to one of the field markers as shown in **Stage 2**. From here on, she is to remain on the imaginary line and dribble to the next field marker as shown in **Stage 3** by the Group 2 players (adjacent players). After arriving at the next field marker, she is to head back towards the first field marker and then to the middle of the imaginary line before passing the ball off to her teammate. *Note:* The dribbler will dribble pass a total of three field markers before passing off the ball.

> While dribbling the ball to the field markers, the dribbling player must keep the ball screened from her opponent.
>
> The opponent must stay on his side of the imaginary line. This is restrictive for the opponent, but necessary to enable the dribbling player to gain confidence while applying the shielding technique.

- After this player has dribbled the ball back to the middle, she is then to pass the ball to the teammate between the other field markers, with a brisk pass. The process is then repeated by the second set of teammates.

- After both of the dribbling/shielding teammates have completed their exercise once, the players are to switch roles, i.e., the dribbling players now become the defenders and vice versa.

- The duration of this drill should be 15 minutes.

- **During this drill, the coach should determine that the dribbling player is successfully shielding the ball and also that the opponent is not crossing the imaginary line.**

Drill 2.6
PUSH-PASS

The Mechanics

The Push-Pass Kick is shown in *Illustration 2-5* (see previous page). It is not a kick that is made in the normal sense of the word kick. As the name implies, it is actually a pass (or kick) pushed by the foot just above the arch as can be seen in the illustration. The Push-Pass is made by the player squatting just before the kick. The non kicking foot and knee are pointed towards the target and are bent at about 20 degrees.

During the Push-Pass Kick, the players must keep their eyes on the ball during the entire kicking process and follow through the kick to maintain an accurate pass or shot on the goal.

The Drills

Version 1 (Static Situation)

This drill is performed in the same manner as Drill 2.1, *Version 1* except that the Push-Pass Kick is substituted for the *static* version of the Basic Instep Kick.

Version 2 (Dynamic Situation)

This drill is performed in the same manner as Drill 2.1, *Version 2* except that the Push-Pass Kick is substituted for the *dynamic* version of the Basic Instep Kick.

Drill 2.7

THE UNDER-THE-FOOT TRAP AND AN INTRODUCTION TO SHIELDING-WHILE-TRAPPING

The Mechanics

The Under-the-Foot Trap is shown in *Illustration 2-6*. This trap is made when a ball is coming straight towards a player: It is generally an easy trap to make when the ball is rolling on the ground. It is more difficult to make this trap when the ball is coming from the air to the player and drops to the ground at foot level; but with practice, it can be mastered. However the trapping of air balls is beyond the scope of this drill.

This trap is especially useful in indoor soccer and thus has more application for the skillful players, but this drill is designed to add the introduction to shielding-while-trapping. It is

***Illustration* 2-6.** The Under-the-Foot Trap. The ball is trapped by forming a wedge between the ground and the underside of the foot.

beneficial for young and inexperienced players to perform this trap as they are introduced to shielding while trapping. Only rolling-grounders are to be kicked to the trapping player.

Note: A distinction must be made here as to when a player may or may not shield the ball. If a player has an opponent at her back before a trap is to be made, and both may be running to trap the ball, a natural screening is taking place, i.e. the player reaching the ball first has a player at her back at the time of the trap. This natural screening of the ball is permissible. However, a player is not permitted to place her body between the opponent and ball if she is not in possession of it, say when both players are alongside of the ball. With this drill, the opponent is at the back of the trapping player when the trap is made.

The trap is made, during this drill, with the player facing the moving ball. As the ball comes towards the player, she is to go to it and stop just before making the trap. The player then puts out her foot and wedges the ball between the sole of the shoe and the ground. During the trap the player must keep her eyes on the ball. It must be noted that this trap is not too useful when an opponent is in front of or at the side of the trapping player; however, when an opponent is to the player's rear, it is naturally shielded during the trapping and relatively easy to be performed correctly. This drill uses an opponent to the trapper's rear and he is to stay to the rear of the trapper during the trap, adding only a relatively slight amount of pressure

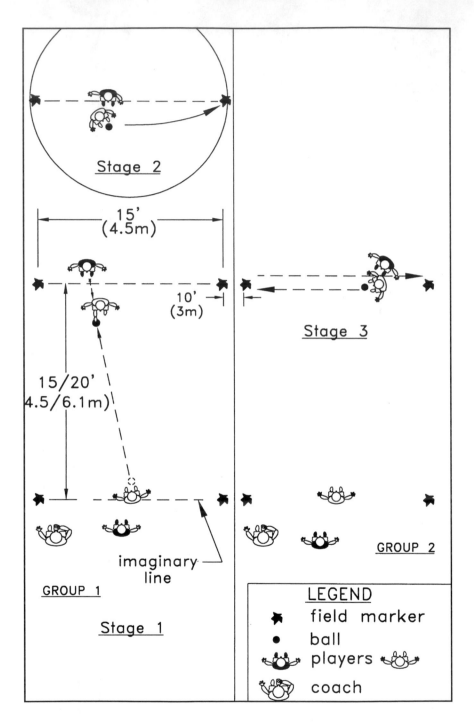

Stage 2

15'
(4.5m)

10'
(3m)

Stage 3

15/20'
(4.5/6.1m)

imaginary
line

GROUP 1

Stage 1

GROUP 2

LEGEND
★ field marker
● ball
players
coach

*Figure 2-6. The Under-the-Foot Trap
and an Introduction to Shielding-While-Trapping Drill*

during the trap. After the trap, the player with the ball is to turn to one of the field markers and dribble the ball up to it. When the dribbler reaches the first field marker the opponent is to begin applying more pressure at the back of the dribbler. The dribbling player is then to dribble the ball to the other field marker and back to the first field marker, then to the middle before kicking it to her teammate. During this dribbling part of the drill, the ball is to be screened from the opponent while the opponent is trying to remove it from the dribbler. The opponent may not cross the imaginary line made by the field markers. This is the same process as performed in the Basic Shielding-While-Dribbling Drill.

The Drill

- Set up the drill as shown in *Figure 2-6*. This figure shows only two of many groups of players spaced 10' (3 m) apart. For this discussion, we will only be initially concerned with Group 1, containing four players. The players in similar jerseys are on the same team. The field markers separate the players by 15' to 20' (4.5 m to 6 m), depending upon their age and abilities. These markers signify an imaginary line that constrains the players. The players with the light jerseys may only move along this line when dribbling and the players in the dark jerseys may only move along the line while trying to tackle the ball from their opponents; however, they will move forward of the line during the trapping process.

- The first player of Group 1 passes the ball to the teammate, she (the player in the light jersey) is to move to the ball (a few feet in front of the line) and trap it as shown in **Stage 1**. The opponent is to apply a slight amount of pressure from the rear only.

- After the ball is under the control of the trapping player she is to dribble back to one of the field markers as shown in **Stage 2**. During this time, the opponent is to reduce his pressure until they arrive back on this imaginary line

- As shown in Group 2, she is to dribble the ball to the next field marker, then to the next field marker before returning back towards the middle as shown in **Stage 3**. *Note:* The dribbler will dribble past a total of three field markers before passing off the ball.

    While dribbling the ball to the field markers the dribbling player must keep the ball screened from her opponent.

During this part of the drill the opponent is to endeavor to tackle the ball from the dribbling player, but cannot cross the line to do so. This is important for instilling confidence in the dribbling, shielding player: Too much pressure upon a novice player will make the shielding process difficult to learn.

- After this player has dribbled the ball back to the middle, she is then to pass the ball to the teammate between the other field markers, with a brisk pass. The process is then repeated by the second set of teammates.

- After both of the dribbling/shielding teammates have completed their exercise once, the players are to switch roles, i.e., the dribbling players now become the defenders and vice versa.

- The duration of this drill should be 15 minutes.

- **During this drill, the coach should determine that the dribbling player is successfully shielding the ball and also that the opponent is not crossing the imaginary line.**

Drill 2.8
HEADING

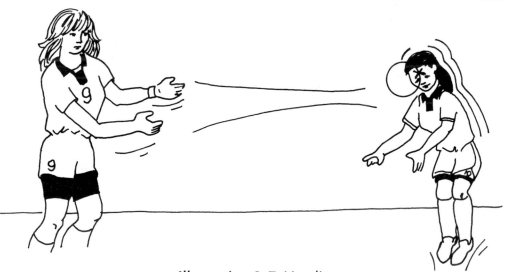

Illustration 2-7. Heading

The Mechanics

Heading a soccer ball is performed by propelling the ball with the back and neck. See *Illustration 2-7*. The ball is contacted at the lower center of the forehead with the eyes open and on the ball at all times. With the back and neck in a rearward position, the ball is then struck with the center of the forehead as the back and neck are thrust forward to meet the ball. Keeping one's eyes open during the time of contact is difficult for novice soccer players; therefore, the ball should be thrown to these players at a moderate speed. As players progress with this skill, they can receive faster balls.

The Drill

- Arrange the players as shown in *Figure 2-7* (see page 44). The distance can vary depending upon the players' age and abilities.

- The coach is to throw the ball, starting at the knee level, underhanded using both hands. The player is to head the ball back to the coach, parallel to the ground or downwards. If the ball rises more than 15 degrees from the horizontal, the ball has been headed incorrectly for this drill.

- Each player will get to head the ball three times, if done correctly, before returning to the end of the line. If the heading is not done correctly or the throws are imprecise, repeat each throw until each player gets to head the ball three times correctly. *Note:* This drill has purposefully not been designed for efficiency utilizing two players: The coach is to throw the ball and must carefully watch each player to determine that the heading is done correctly. If an assistant coach is available, give him or her proper instruction as to what to watch out for and utilize this individual in a second drill group.

- After three good heads the player is to return to the end of the line. If an assistant coach is utilized, the players will switch to the alternate lines.

- The drill should last for 15 minutes with each player having taken an equal number of turns.

- **The coach is to observe that the player gets to propel the ball using the back and neck, keeps her eyes open, and contacts the ball with the forehead, and that the ball is headed back to the coach either parallel to the ground or downwards.**

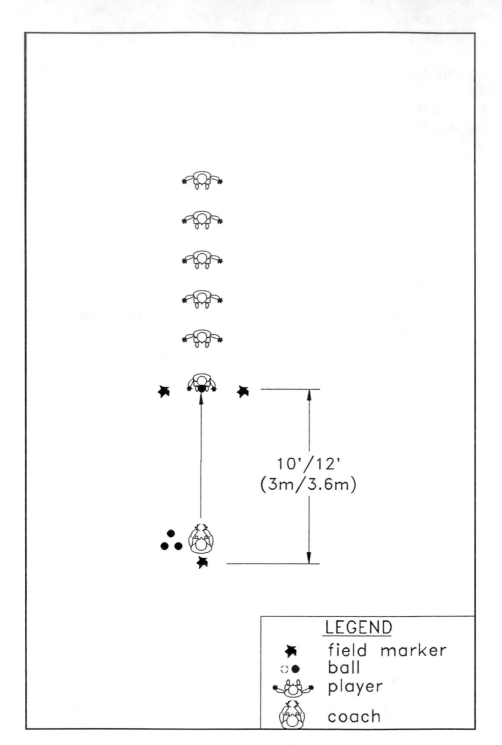

LEGEND

✹	field marker
◌●	ball
🤸	player
🧍	coach

Figure 2-7. The Heading Drill

10'/12'
(3m/3.6m)

Drill 2.9
THE BASIC THROW-IN DRILL

The Mechanics

When the ball crosses the touch line, a throw-in is awarded to the team that did not touch the ball last prior to it going out of bounds. Very often with amateur teams the throw-in is more advantageous to the opponents, because the ultimate outcome of the throw-in often ends up with the ball in the opponents' possession. Possession of the ball should be the object of the play, but by reviewing many throw-in situations one might question the advantage of a throw-in.

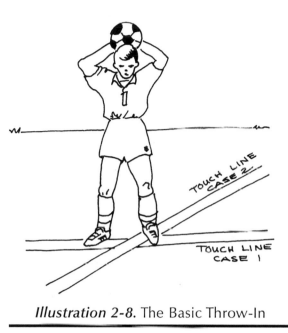

Illustration 2-8. The Basic Throw-In

There are many ways to make throw-ins and most of them are disadvantageous. When teams take a non-disciplined approach to making throw-ins, the ball can end up in possession of the other team due to the thrower's illegal motions, bad judgment or opponent pressure. Mistakes are difficult to avoid when a thrower typically takes a running start to seemingly get more power into the throw. The fact remains that the running start generally gives very little, if any additional velocity to the ball due to the abrupt stop of the thrower at the touch line. This running start frequently causes a player to favor one arm during the throw, have a foot in the air, or throw in a direction different than the one that the thrower is facing. These motions are illegal while making a throw-in. Another problem also occurs when the ball is thrown up the line to seemingly gain some yardage. This move is proscribed. Opponents usually congregate up the line, so the throw should not take place there. Lastly, it is not an easy task for a receiver to settle the ball under the opponent pressure ordinarily accompanying throw-ins. This drill covers the most effective technique for making a good throw-in, but it does not address the receiving player's problem. This problem is covered in Chapter 6.

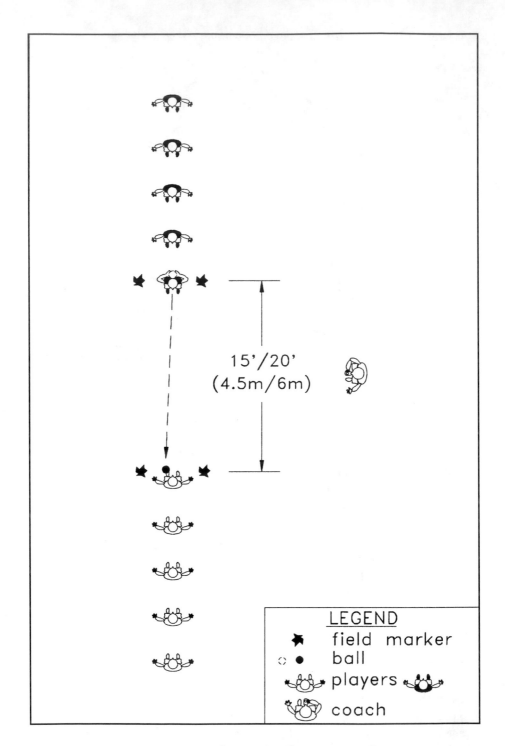

LEGEND
★ field marker
○ ● ball
players
coach

Figure 2-8. The Basic Throw-In Drill

The procedure in this drill requires that players make throw-ins while remaining stationary while standing on or behind the touch line. *Illustration 2-8* (see page 45) shows a player making a throw from a stationary position, showing the player's correct feet positions described as Case 1 and Case 2. The foot or feet may be on the touch line (case 1) or behind it (case 2) during the throw. To make a legal throw-in and to comply with the procedure of this drill, the thrower is to face the receiver, place the ball totally behind the head and throw it with two hands, with equal power coming from both arms and the back, all the while remaining in a stationary position facing the receiver. It is also necessary to release the ball only after it passes over the face and to maintain both feet on the ground during the entire procedure.

In summary, remaining stationary during the throw nearly insures that the throw will be acceptable to the referee's judgment as to whether or not the throw has been executed properly and legally. *Note:* Since this drill does not replicate game conditions normally employing several receivers and opponents, it will be necessary for the players to receive an adequate explanation that denounces throws up the line, unless a potential receiver up the line is unmarked.

The Drill

- Set up the drill as shown in *Figure 2-8*. The throwing distance may be adjusted according to the age level or players' throwing abilities.

- Each player at the head of the line is to throw the ball to the player at the head of the opposite line. The throw is to be made such that it arrives at the feet of the receiver enabling him to easily trap and settle the ball. This is very important. If the throw is poorly made, the throw should be repeated until it is made correctly.

- After the ball is trapped and settled, this trapping player is to pick up the ball and make a throw to the opposing receiver. After each successful throw, the thrower then moves to the end of the opposite line.

- The duration of the drill should be 15 minutes.

- **The coach is to observe that the throws are made legally and that the ball reaches the receiver's feet for easy entrapment and settlement of the ball. The coach is to also observe whether or not the receiver is trapping and settling the ball correctly.**

2b. Basic Field Drills— Defensive

Drill 2.10

Basic Backing-Up Defense Drill

Illustration 2-9. Basic Backing-Up Defense Drill. The correct defensive move is to remain balanced on one's toes and to back up with the attacker; and never commit oneself to a tackle until the attacker has lost control of the ball.

The Mechanics

This technique is used to control the advance of an opponent dribbling the ball down field. The word "control" is key here. A defending player need not gain possession of the ball to exercise this move properly or to benefit the team. To win soccer games, proper defensive measures are crucial such as controlling the advance of a dribbling opponent: This is a very effective tactic.

The move described here is so simple, yet it is very often overlooked by many teams, especially losing teams—even at the professional level. This move is often misunderstood and mistakenly assumed to be a defending player problem or error, but many goals can be prevented when it is employed properly.

Review scored goals on TV. If one has a video tape of the moments prior to the scored goals, one can often see defensive mistakes by players attempting to make a Standing Block Tackle—even at the professional level. With slow-motion replay, it can often be observed that one or several defenders are guilty of making unsuccessful tackles. Thus these players are indirectly responsible for goals being scored against their teams. Yet players making these serious defensive errors are seldom held accountable for their mistakes. However, knowledgeable soccer players do recognize good defensive playing: I have personally been given credit for my defensive-wing playing in several games, even though many times throughout those games I did not come into contact with the ball.

Illustration 2-9 shows a defending player controlling the motion of an attacking player. The defending player is backing up with the attacker maintaining the proper distance from him. The proper distance comes about by not being too close to allow the attacker to accelerate past the defending player nor being too far to allow for a clear pass or a clear shot on goal. This distance depends upon the potential speed of both players and with recent practice, and experience, the distance becomes known to the defender. However, after just a few weeks of being out of practice, a player's judgment here may wane.

The correct defensive posture is to back up with a dribbling player, keeping balance and doing so on the toes. This way, with each change in the dribbler's direction, the defending player is able to remain in front of him. The defender is to keep her eyes on the ball at all times and not be tricked into going for the ball or for the tackle. It must be remembered that as long as the dribbling player has control of the ball it is extremely difficult to remove it from him. The dribbling player must be contained with the proper distance by the defender. This action can continue up to location D* (see *Figure 2-9*) in front of the goal. At this point the defender must

*Since this drill does not use a goalkeeper, the small goal is used and the distance D is located 5' (1.5m) from the goal. This distance should be about 10' (3 m) when using a regulation goal and a goalkeeper.

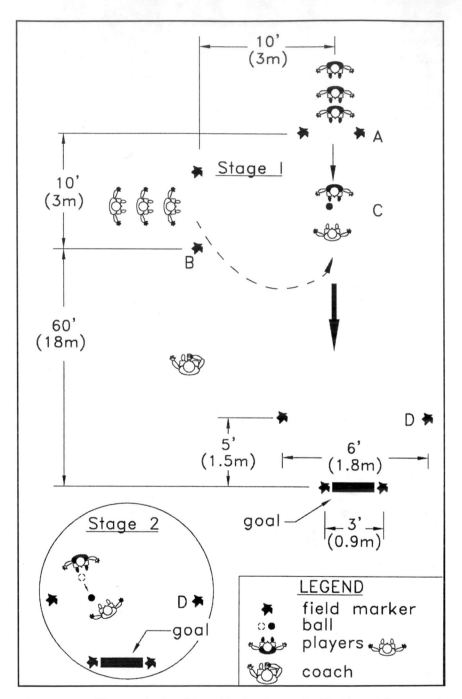

10'
(3m)

A

Stage I

10'
(3m)

C

B

60'
(18m)

D

5'
(1.5m)

6'
(1.8m)

goal

3'
(0.9m)

Stage 2

D

goal

LEGEND

field marker
ball
players
coach

Figure 2-9. The Basic Backing-Up Defense Drill. Note: The coach is to be convinced that this procedure is absolutely correct before presenting this drill to players.

hold her ground and let the attacking player make his move. It is also advisable that the defending player control the motion of a dribbling player in such a way as to force this attacker out towards the wings; thus further reducing the danger of having this player take a shot directly in front of the goal.

The Drill

Stage 1

- Set up the drill according to *Figure 2-9* and note the markers at position D: They are at the point where the defender is to hold the line as she is to stop the retreating motion. This drill is performed with two players (an attacker and a defender). The attacking player begins dribbling from the line located at A. The defending player emerges from the line located at B. Both players meet at Location C.

- The attacker is to advance towards the goal maintaining full control of the ball. The defender is to back up with the attacker with a posture described above.

- The defender is not to commit herself unless the attacker loses control of the ball and she is positive that she can get to the ball.

Stage 2

- The players are to advance towards the small goal until the defender reaches the field markers located at D. At this point, she is to hold her ground and wait for the attacker to make the next move. *Reminder:* If the attacker tricks the defender into going for the tackle and she mistackles the ball, the attacker will most likely be in an advantageous position for a clear shot at the goal.

- If the attacker moves laterally, the defender is to maintain her goal-distance and move in the same direction.

- At this point, there should be an attempt to score. After the shot, the attacker is to retrieve the ball, return it to Location C and go to the end of the line located at B. The defender then goes to the end of the line located at A.

- Do this drill for 15 minutes.

- The coach should be observing that the attacker is contained, not be preoccupied as to whether or not the defender removes the ball from the attacker or whether or not a goal is scored in the process: If a goalkeeper were in place, there is a good chance that this person would stop any shot on goal.

- It is important that the other players observe the drills as they take place and take note of successful defenses as well as any unsuccessful attempts to dislodge the ball from the attacker.

- During games, the coach should caution any friendly spectators not to shout to the defenders, "Get the ball."

Drill 2.11

PRELIMINARY SHIELDING IMMEDIATELY AFTER TRAPPING

The Mechanics

Preliminary Shielding Immediately After Trapping is another shielding drill that progressively receives greater opponent pressure. This is the third of five drills that involves shielding. *Note:* Even though shielding is performed in the offensive state, it is a natural defensive measure and therefore some of the drills containing shielding will be found in either category.

This trapping process has similarities to the Under-the-Foot Trapping and Introduction to Shielding While Dribbling Drill, except that there are no constraints as to where the players may move to and full pressure is applied only after any type of trap is made. The drill proceeds in this manner with reference to *Figure 2-10*. A ball is passed to the trapping player at Location C by the coach located at A. This is **Stage 1**. The trapper moves to the ball at Location D, traps it and gets it under control (the trap may be made with any desired type of trap). Simultaneously, the opponent located at B runs in the direction of the trapping player, applying pressure, but the opponent distance is set such that the arrival time is just after the trapping player gets the ball under his control, as shown in **Stage 2**.

As the opponent arrives near the trapping player (having arrived just after the ball is under control of the trapping player), the trapping player turns by placing his back to the opponent. This is **Stage 3**. This move causes

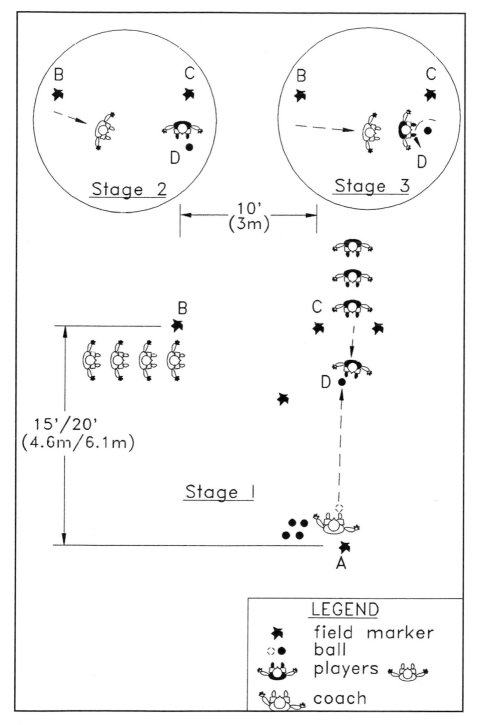

Figure 2-10. Preliminary Shielding Immediately After Trapping

the player with the ball to position himself such that his body is between the opponent and the ball, and is fully shielding it from the opponent. With the opponent now at his back and applying pressure, he (the dribbler) dribbles in a straight line away from the opponent while keeping peripheral vision on him. Taking about three or four dribbling steps, the dribbling player then passes the ball back to the coach while still screening the ball, i.e., the kick back to the coach is made with the foot furthest from the opponent. The drill is now completed. *Note:* Novice players may have difficulty kicking with the non-favored foot: The drill instills into them the advantage of kicking with both feet.

Stage 1

- Set up the drill as shown *Figure 2-10* (see previous page). The coach is located at A. There are two lines of players at right angles to each other. The players located at C are the trapping players and the players located B are the opponents.

- At the start of the drill, the coach kicks a ball to the player initially located at C. This player moves to the ball and stops just before trapping the ball at about location D.

Stage 2

- At the same time as the ball is kicked, an opponent from the line located at B runs towards the player who is arriving at location D with the purpose of tackling the ball from the trapping player. The spacing between the players is such that there is enough time for the trapping player to settle the ball. If the opponent arrives too soon or too late, the distance should be adjusted. For this drill, it is better for all opponents to arrive a little late than too soon as the purpose is to teach players to shield the ball after it is under their control.

Stage 3

- The player with the ball is then to move around the ball such that his back is to the opponent. The trapping player is then to shield the ball against the defender's pressure and dribble it for several steps to his front while preventing the opponent from getting near the ball.

- After the dribbling player has demonstrated that he has shielded the ball and has it under his control, he is to pass it back to the coach with a foot that is the most shielded from the opponent. If the pass is blocked or partially blocked by the opponent, the player has not grasped the purpose of shielding the ball. **The purpose must be re-stated by the coach that a truly shielded ball cannot be intercepted by an opponent at any time. If this shielding process is done incorrectly, repeat the drill with the same two players until successful.**

- The trapping player is to join the rear of opponent line and the other player is to join the rear of the trapping line.

- **During this drill, the coach should be observing that the trapping player goes to the ball, stops and then performs the trap correctly while keeping his eyes on the ball.**

- **Also during this drill, the coach should be observing that the dribbling player is successfully shielding the ball and that the pass back to the coach is made such that the opponent has no chance of blocking it.**

3a. Goalkeeping Drills— Basic

A Note to the Coach and Assistant Coach

During the normal drills for the field players (without the use of a goal-keeper), it is most efficient and practical for the coach to utilize an assistant coach in the training of the goalkeeper. This is preferred over having the goalkeeper(s) participate in all field drills. This method will be efficient when following these guidelines:

- It is not important for the assistant coach to have soccer experience as long as this individual can throw the ball in a prescribed manner and observe the training principles outlined by the coach.

- Prior to the session's training, it is recommended that the coach practice the drills-for-the-day with the assistant coach and goalkeeper(s) for five to ten minutes.

- It must be clear that these are exercises for the goalkeeper's training and not for the assistant coach to practice kicking.

- A ball propelled by hand has the same effect as a kicked ball, but is more consistent; consequently, it is a more efficient training method.

- The ideal location of many of the throws will be at a point that will make the goalkeeper work the hardest. When the assistant coach is working with the goalkeeper(s), he will naturally make some throwing errors, i.e., ones that are either too easy or too difficult to save. He is to repeat the throws to the goalkeeper as many times as necessary to enable the goalkeeper to make several difficult saves located at the end of his reach.

Goalkeeping Drills

There are numerous drills for training goalkeepers, but the most efficient are the ones that have direct application to game situations. Drills that supposedly promote dexterity may be useful, but usually do not utilize

Illustration 3-1. The Goalkeeper's Stance

the goalkeeper's time wisely. While there are many schools of thought on drills best utilized by goalkeepers, the method presented here recommends that novice goalkeepers be subjected to the same routine drills presented in this text for two consecutive years (or two seasons). If the goalkeeper(s) are well schooled in these drills for a minimum of two soccer seasons, other drills can be introduced after this novice training period. It is strongly urged that the goalkeeper(s) reiterate these drills because the goalkeeping skills must become conditional responses rather than conscious actions. These reactions include, for example: catching the ball, bringing up the knee when jumping, deciding whether to use tipping or catching, keeping the legs together for rolling balls, keeping the eyes focused on the ball, etc. They should become automatic as there is no substitute for repetition. These basics may otherwise be overlooked if the goalkeeper is constantly practicing different drills and techniques. In addition, regardless of the physical skills needed by goalkeepers, sensitivity to the team's needs, both defensive and offensive, are also necessary. They must also be taught and cultivated. As the goalkeeper becomes dexterous in physical skills, he or she will gradually be introduced to sophisticated defensive and offensive measures covered later in this text.

The goalkeeper's normal stance is shown in *Illustration 3-1.* The position for readiness is to be standing about 4' to 5' (1.2 to 1.5 m) centered in front of the goal relative to the ball. If the opponent's offensive move is coming to either side, the goalkeeper normally moves in that direction, but remains generally about the same distance in front of the goal, unless there is a breakaway. In this case, the goalkeeper would move out further to reduce the exposed area of the goal (cut down the angles on either side of the goal).

While expecting activity in and around the goal area, she should be standing on her toes with the legs closed sufficiently to deflect any shot that could pass between the legs. The arms should be extended out somewhat to reduce the target area with the body leaning slightly forward. The face and body should portray confidence as any sign of fear by the goalkeeper will be conveyed to the attacker at the time the shot is taken. *Note:* While some goalies prefer to stand with the legs further apart, it makes sense to utilize them as a blockade by closing them up to less then the ball's width. This posture could prevent an unexpected shot from slipping between the legs.

Drill 3.1

TIPPING THE BALL OVER THE TOP OF THE GOAL

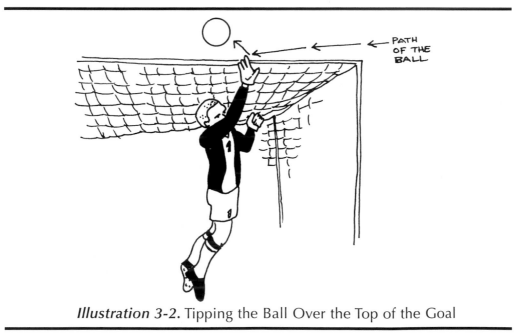

Illustration 3-2. Tipping the Ball Over the Top of the Goal

The Mechanics

This is the first of three of the goalkeeper's noncatching techniques. This method of tipping or deflecting the ball over the crossbar is an elementary technique because it can be employed immediately by novice goalkeepers not yet skilled in catching the ball. Yet, it is a very useful skill for an experienced goalkeeper to master. At advanced levels of soccer, shots at the goal may be kicked hard and high, and with large amounts of spin make them difficult to catch. *Illustration 3-2* shows the correct way a goalkeeper deflects a ball over the top of the goal crossbar. He is reaching for the ball that is out of range for a safe catch and is tipping the ball with his fingertips. The incorrect way of tipping the ball would be to slow it down with the full or partial surface of fingers or hand. If the ball is not deflected, but slowed down, it can drop behind the goalkeeper and into the goal.

During this procedure, if the ball is high and to the left or right of the goalkeeper, he is to jump off of the ball of the opposite foot to the hand deflecting the ball. He is also to keep his eyes on the ball at all times by following it over the crossbar.

The Drill

- It is best to practice this drill with a regulation size outdoor goal and if at all possible, do this drill in front of a goal with a net. *Figure 3-1* (see page 60) shows a goalkeeper and his coach in front of the goal just after the throw from the coach. The goalkeeper's position is about 4' to 5' (1.2 m to 1.5 m) in front of the goal, midway between the goal posts, prior to the throw.

- Prior to the goalkeeper performing this exercise, he should precondition himself with jumps without the ball. Have the goalkeeper leap off the ground from the ball of the foot with ten repetitions from the right foot, then ten repetitions from the left foot. While doing so on the **right foot**, he is to reach up with his **left hand** stretched overhead and to the **left** and similarly with the **right hand** while leaping off of the **left foot**. Even though there is no ball used for the pre-conditioning, the goalkeeper is to look up at his hand during the jump to practice keeping his eyes on the ball.

- With the goalkeeper ready for the drill, the assistant coach places himself about 15' (4.6 m) in front of him. This distance will vary

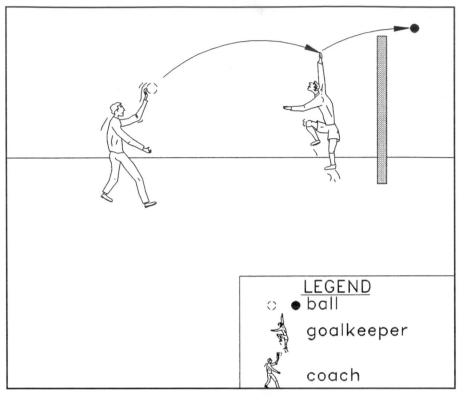

Figure 3-1. Tipping the Ball Over the Top of the Goal Drill

depending upon the goalkeeper's age and skill level. *Note:* It is the assistant coach's job to throw the ball over the goalkeeper's head such that it could score a goal if the goalkeeper does not jump up and deflect the ball with the finger tips. The throws are to be directly overhead, and off to both sides of the goalkeeper who must jump and stretch for all tip-overs. The goalkeeper is to keep his eyes on the ball during the jumping part of the drill.

• If this is the first time that this drill is being performed, after about ten successful tip-overs each with the left and the right hand, it is instructive for the goalkeeper to have some goals scored by doing this exercise incorrectly. The correct method is to deflect the ball without slowing down its speed. The incorrect method is to slow the ball down by using the whole fingers or whole fingers along with the palm to slow the ball down (not deflect it). When done incorrectly, the ball will pass over the goalkeeper, but frequently under the crossbar.

- The length of the drill should be ten minutes.

- **The assistant coach should be watching that the goalkeeper is jumping up from the ball of the right foot for a left handed tip-over and vice versa for the left foot. He is also to observe that the ball is deflected, not reduced in speed and that the eyes are following the ball as it is guided over the crossbar.**

Drill 3.2
TIPPING THE BALL
OVER THE SIDE OF THE GOAL

The Mechanics

This is the second of three of the noncatching modes. This technique of tipping or deflecting the ball by the side of the goalpost is another elementary technique because it can be employed immediately by novice goalkeepers not yet skilled in catching the ball safely. It is most useful when used by experienced goalkeepers that are endeavoring to save the ball from a goal, but it is out of reach, possibly slippery, or when the ball is traveling exceptionally fast.

As in Drill 3.1, the incorrect way of tipping the ball would be to slow it down with the fingers or hand. If the ball is not deflected, but slowed down, it can drop behind the goalkeeper and glide into the goal. It may also just stop and lie in front of the goal waiting for some attacker to take advantage of the situation. During this procedure, the goalkeeper must leap off to the side to tip the ball out safely to the side of the upright goalpost. He is to keep his eyes on the ball at all times.

The Drill

- It is best to practice this drill with a regulation size outdoor goal and, if at all possible, do this drill in front of a goal with a net. *Figure 3-2* (see page 62) shows a goalkeeper deflecting the ball after it has been thrown by the assistant coach. The goalkeeper is to be normally standing about 4' to 5' (1.2 m 1.5 m) in front of the goal, midway between the goal posts, waiting for the throw from the assistant coach.

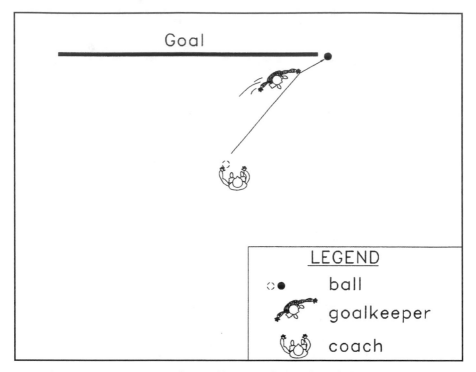

Figure 3-2. Tipping the Ball Over the Side of the Goal Drill

- Prior to the goalkeeper performing this exercise and as in the previous exercise, he should precondition himself with jumps without the ball. Have the goalkeeper leap off the ground from the ball of the foot with ten repetitions from the right foot, then ten repetitions from the left foot. While doing so on the **right foot**, he is to reach out with his **left hand** stretched in the direction of his **left upright goalpost** and similarly with the **right hand** while leaping off of the **left foot**. Even though there is no ball used for the pre-conditioning, the goalkeeper is to look out at his hand during the jump to practice keeping his eyes in the direction of the ball.

- With the goalkeeper ready for the drill, the assistant coach places himself about 15' (4.6 m) in front of the him. This distance will vary depending upon the goalkeeper's age and skill level. *Note:* It is the assistant coach's job to throw the ball to the side of goalkeeper's reach such that it could score a goal if the goalkeeper does not leap to the side and deflect the ball with the finger tips. The goalkeeper is to keep his eyes on the ball's flight during the jumping part of the drill.

- If this is the first time that this drill is being performed, after about ten successful tip-over-the-sides with the left and the right hand each, it is instructive for the goalkeeper to have some goals scored by doing this exercise incorrectly, by slowing down the speed of the ball. The correct method is to deflect the ball without slowing its speed. The incorrect method is to slow the ball down by using the whole fingers or whole fingers along with the palm. When done incorrectly, the ball will pass to the side of the goalkeeper, but not outside the upright posts of the goal: It will score by going between the goalkeeper and inside the upright post.

- Repeat the correct drill for ten minutes.

- **The assistant coach should be watching that the goalkeeper is jumping up from the ball of the right foot for a left handed leap and vice versa for the left foot. He is also to observe that the ball is deflected, not slowed down, and that the eyes are on the ball during the jumping process.**

Drill 3.3
PUNCHING THE BALL

The Mechanics

This is the third of three of the three noncatching modes. This invaluable technique of punching the ball is an elementary technique because it can be employed immediately by novice goalkeepers not yet skilled in catching the ball. It is most useful when employed by experienced goalkeepers. It is an exceptional technique when used skillfully to save balls that are hit hard, have a high degree of spin, are wet, or when there is traffic in the goal area, i.e., the ball is out of reach for a safe catch or in a crowded goal area where it could be physically hazardous for the goalkeeper to catch the ball. This technique is performed with either one or both hands. *Illustration 3-3* shows a goalkeeper punching a ball out of harm's

Illustration 3-3. Punching the Ball

way. He is using two fists to punch the ball that is out of range for a safe catch.

The correct way to make a double fisted punch is to bring both hands together and punch outward and upwards. It can also be performed using a single fist when the ball is out of reach for a two-fisted punch. In either case, assure that the thumb or thumbs are tucked in for protection (the thumb tips are to be below the middle knuckle of the index finger(s). The ball must be punched out of the goal area, slightly elevated and directed as far away from the goal as possible to prevent another immediate shot at the goal (the incorrect way of punching the ball would be to punch it out near the center of the field or low to the ground). During this procedure, the goalkeeper must keep his eyes on the ball and ordinarily jump off of the ball of the opposite foot of the hand punching the ball when reaching and performing a single-fisted punch. The punch can be made off of a two-footed jump when the ball is approximately directly overhead or made near the goalkeeper's standing position. It is paramount to not perform this tentatively. The goalkeeper must decide that he is to get the ball at all costs and must not perform this technique in a haphazard manner.

The Drill

- It is best to practice this drill with a regulation size outdoor goal and, if at all possible, do this drill in front of a goal with a net. *Figure 3-3* shows a goalkeeper and his assistant coach in front of the goal just after the throw from the assistant coach. The goalkeeper's position is about 4' to 5' (1.2 m to 1.5 m) in front of the goal, midway between the goal posts, before the throw from the assistant coach.

- Prior to the goalkeeper performing this exercise, he should precondition himself with jumps without the ball. Have the goalkeeper leap off the ground from the balls of both feet with ten repetitions as if punching a ball directly overhead. He should also make ten repetitions each for single fisted punches to his right and left. While doing so he is to punch the air as if there is a ball in front of his fists. Even though there is no ball used for the pre-conditioning, the goalkeeper is to look up at his hands during the jump to practice keeping his eyes on the ball.

- With the goalkeeper ready for the drill, the assistant coach places himself about 15' (4.6 m) in front of the him. This distance will

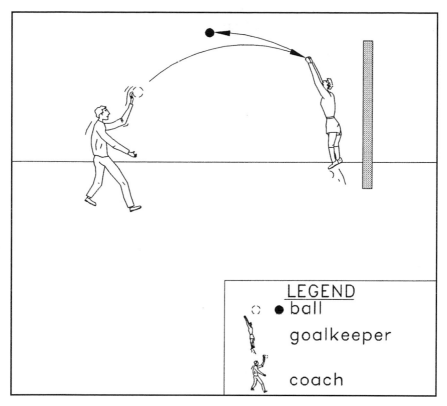

Figure 3-3. Punching the Ball Drill

vary depending upon the goalkeeper's age and skill level. *Note 1:* It is the assistant coach's job to throw the ball above the goalkeeper's head such that it could score a goal if the goalkeeper does not jump up and punch it (out towards one of the touchlines). The throws are to be directly overhead, and off to both sides of the goalkeeper who must jump and stretch to make single fisted punch-outs. The goalkeeper is to keep his eyes on the ball during the jumping part of the drill. *Note 2:* Should the student goalkeeper incorrectly punch the ball to the assistant coach or not be assertive with the punching, the coach should kick the ball into the goal.

- **The assistant coach should be watching that the goalkeeper is jumping up from the balls of his feet for the front double fisted punch-outs and off the right foot for a left handed punch-out and vice versa for the left foot and right hand. He is also to observe that the ball is directed away from the middle of the field.**

Drill 3.4

Catching Air Balls

Illustration 3-4. Catching Air Balls Hand Position. The position of the hands is shown before the catch is made. *Illustration 3-4* shows the hands position for high level balls.

The Mechanics

Part 1 (Catches Above the Waist)

This technique, catching the ball above the waist, is employed by goalkeepers when they are sure of the catch. If possible, the body is placed behind the ball to align it perpendicular to its flight. This gives one an added measure of security for the catch. After the ball is caught, it is brought into the midsection or chest. The arms and hands should wrap around the ball as the goalkeeper must clutch it for maximum security. This procedure is performed at all times even for the simplest of catches.

Illustration 3-4 shows a goalkeeper's hands: They form a "W" for catching kicked or headed balls above the waist. The thumbs are shown located behind the ball for stability. While the catch is made with the hands, it must be instilled into the novice goalkeeper that the ball is not fully caught until it is protected by the whole body such as with the hands, arms and chest or midsection. The midsection is the most secure place for the ball after the catch is made.

Illustration 3-5 shows a goalkeeper in the air after catching the ball at midbody level. Note that one knee is elevated during the catch. Goalkeepers need to apply this measure of protection for themselves to intimidate any possibly aggressive opponents that could come too close to them while they are most vulnerable, i.e., in the air. *Note 1:* This must be done while catching the ball, not after.

When returning the ball to the assistant coach, the goalkeeper should practice bowling the ball to the coach's feet. *Note 2*: Before returning the ball to the coach the goalkeeper should practice looking around as if he is in an actual game situation.

The Drill

Illustration 3-5
The Air Ball Catch
The goalkeeper is shown making a midbody catch while in the air.

- It is best to practice this drill with a regulation size outdoor goal and, if at all possible, do this drill in front of a goal with a net, but field markers would be sufficient. The goalkeeper should be standing 4' to 5' (1.2 m to 1.5 m) centered in front of the goal.

- Prior to the goalkeeper performing this exercise, he should precondition himself with jumps without the ball. Have the goalkeeper leap off the ground in a similar manner as in Drill 3.1, with ten repetitions to the right and ten repetitions to the left. While doing so he is to catch an imaginary high ball. Even though there is no ball used for the pre-conditioning, the goalkeeper is to look up at his hands during the jump to practice keeping his eyes on the ball.

- With the goalkeeper ready for the drill, the assistant coach places himself about 15' (4.6 m) in front of him. This distance will vary depending upon the goalkeeper's age and skill level. *Note:* It is the assistant coach's job to throw the ball above the goalkeeper's head 15 times. Then directly at the goalkeeper's midsection 15 times.

- Next, the throws are to be directly off to both sides of the goalkeeper, 15 times each. The goalkeeper is to keep his eyes on the ball during the catching part of the drill.

- **The assistant coach should be watching for the following:**

The goalkeeper is jumping up from the balls of his feet in a similar manner as described in Drill 3.1.

The goalkeeper is to align himself perpendicular to the flight of the ball to keep the body directly behind it.

He is to observe that after the ball is caught with the hands, the body is wrapped around the ball as shown in *Illustration 3-5* (see page 67).

He is to observe that the ball is returned properly by determining that the goalkeeper is concentrating on the return throw by observing the field and returning the ball by a bowling type throw. *Note:* Novice goalkeepers often consider the return throw back to their trainer as routine: They need to also concentrate on this aspect of their training.

Part 2 (Catches Below the Waist)

The Mechanics

This technique is for catching low level balls. The goalkeeper is to place the body behind the ball and align it to be perpendicular to its path, if possible: This gives one a measure of security for the catch. After the ball is caught, it is brought into the midsection or chest. The arms and hands should wrap around the ball as the goalkeeper must clutch it to his chest for maximum security. This procedure is performed at all times even for the simplest of catches.

While the catch is made with the hands, it must be constantly instilled into the novice goalkeeper that the ball is not fully caught until it is protected by the whole body, including the hands, arms, chest or midsection just as in high ball catches. The midsection is the most secure place for the ball after the catch is made.

Illustration 3-6 shows a player bending over prior to catching a ground level ball or a low bouncer. The legs are to be closed for this catch and the eyes must be on the ball at all times. It must

Illustration 3-6.
Catching Ground Level Balls

be emphasized that apparently simple catches lower the goaltender's concentration; therefore, full attention must be paid to easy saves.

The Drill

- It is best to practice this drill with a regulation size outdoor goal and, if at all possible, do this drill in front of a goal with a net, but field markers would be sufficient and should be located at a distance equal to the regulation goal width used at this age level. The goalkeeper should be standing 4' to 5' (1.2 m to 1.5 m) centered in front of the goal.

- With the goalkeeper ready for the drill, the assistant coach places himself about 15' (4.6 m) in front of him. This distance will vary depending upon the goalkeeper's age and skill level. *Note:* It is the assistant coach's job to throw the ball to the side of the goalkeeper's left and right legs 15 times each.

- Then throws are directed at the goalkeeper's midsection 15 times.

- He is to repeat this drill with 15 bouncing balls that reach the goalkeeper no higher than the waist.

- Next the throws are to be directly off to both sides of the goalkeeper, 15 times each. The goalkeeper is to keep his eyes on the ball during the catching part of the drill.

- **The assistant coach should be watching for the following:**

  That the goalkeeper is maintaining his legs in a position sufficiently closed to not permit the ball going through them, and that the hands are in the correct position, with the eyes on the ball.

  He is to observe that after the ball is caught with the hands, the body is wrapped around the ball as shown in *Illustration 3-5* (see page 67).

  He is to observe that the ball is returned properly by determining that the goalkeeper is concentrating on the return throw by watching the field and returning the ball by a bowling type throw.

Drill 3.5
Catching Ground Level Balls and Goalkeeper's Throws

The Mechanics

This procedure is for goalkeepers to catch ground balls and low bouncers, and return them to the trainer in a proper manner. As a reminder, the following is repeated from the previous drill for the catch. The goalkeeper is to place the body behind the ball and align it to be perpendicular to the ball's path. After the ball is caught, it is brought into the midsection or chest. The arms and hands should wrap around the ball as the goalkeeper must clutch it for maximum security. This procedure is performed at all times, even for the simplest of catches.

The catches are made at or nearly at ground level. It must be constantly instilled into the novice goalkeeper that while the catch is made the ball is not fully caught until it is protected by the whole body, such as with the hands, arms, or midsection, just as in high ball catches. Refer again to *Illustration 3-6* (see page 68).

Goalkeeper's Throws

During this portion of the drill after the catch, the goalkeeper is to throw the ball back to the assistant coach any of the following three ways. These throws are called the *Low Underhanded Throw,* the *One Hand Overhanded Throw* and the *Two Hand Overhanded Throw.* A simple explanation of the method and uses for these throws should be a sufficient description.

- The *Low Underhanded Throw* is a bowling type throw when it is necessary to make a pass to an open teammate's feet. The goalkeeper simply bowls the soccer ball to the player's feet when the distance is not too great.

- The *One Hand Overhanded Throw* is used to reach a more distant player. This is similar to throwing an oblong (American) football.

- *Two Hand Overhanded Throw* is used to throw the ball to a teammate when it is necessary to throw it over the head of an teammate or an opponent in order to reach a chosen teammate.

The Drill

- This drill may be practiced in front of field markers representing a goal with the goalkeeper standing 4' to 5' (1.2 to 1.5 m) centered in front of this goal.

- With the goalkeeper ready for the drill, the assistant coach places himself about 15' (4.6 m) in front of him. This distance will vary depending upon the goalkeeper's age and skill level. *Note:* It is the assistant coach's job to roll the ball directly at the goalkeeper's feet, 15 times, then to throw 15 low bouncers in the same way.

- Next, the assistant coach is to roll the ball to the side of the goalkeeper's left and right legs 15 times each. When balls are thrown off to the goalkeeper's side, if possible, he is to align himself up with the trajectory prior to making the catch and get behind the ball.

- The goalkeeper is to keep his eyes on the ball while making the catch and to keep his legs closed.

- The goalkeeper is to return the ball in any and all three ways described above.

- **The assistant coach should be watching that the goalkeeper is maintaining his legs in a closed position to not permit the ball going through them. The assistant coach is also to observe that the hands and body become wrapped around the ball at the end of each catch.**

- **Observe that the goalkeeper keeps his eyes on the ball during the catch.**

- **Determine that the return throws are done with care and concentration.**

Drill 3.6

THE GOALKEEPER'S KICK (PUNTING)

The Mechanics

Goalkeepers, especially younger ones, are usually taught to kick the ball up field after catching it, though this is not a desired method of attack

3-7A   3-7B   3-7C

Illustration 3-7. The Goalkeeper's Kick (Punting). *Illustrations 3-7A to 3-7C* show the various stages of the kick.

for ball control soccer. Eventually, the principle of ball control soccer must be impressed upon the whole team such that they should, whenever possible, utilize the thrown ball technique. This is not an easy task for young players or unskilled ball handlers, so kicking the ball up field will temporally be their common mode for launching counter attacks. With time, this counterattack kicking method is to be replaced mostly by a bowling throw to the feet.

The goalkeeper's kick must be practiced frequently to attain distance and accuracy. The punting drill is performed with a goalkeeper or goalkeepers and an assistant coach. The correct method for punting is shown in *Illustration 3-7.* The assistant coach and one or two goalkeepers stand apart from each other (three persons would form a triangle), to kick the ball back and forth to each other at a distance of the maximum kick range of the goalkeeper(s).

Prior to the kick, the goalkeeper is bent over like a question mark and the ball is held at groin level and about 12" (30 cm) away from the body as shown in *Illustration 3-7A.* For a right-footed kick, the left foot should be slightly forward and vise versa for a left-footed kick. The knee of the right leg is brought up such that the calf is bent about 60 to 90 degrees in reference to the ground, see *Illustration 3-7B.* The ball is then *dropped* while the eyes are kept on the ball. After the ball has dropped a few inches (about 15 cm), it is kicked with the bony part of the foot instep, see *Illustration 3-7C. Note:* Most of the kicking power comes from the knee while the kicking leg follows through with the kick as the ball is met with the top of the shoe laces. It is important that the head and eyes are kept facing down for a moment, after the kick, to prevent looking away from the ball and miskicking it to one side to the other.

The Drill

- The goalkeeper's kick should be performed continuously for 10 minutes anywhere on the practice field away from the distraction of the other practicing players. The assistant coach and the goalkeeper(s) should practice this together.
- **The coach should observe that the goalkeeper keeps his eyes on the ball during the entire kicking process and that the kick is followed through.**

Drill 3.7
LUNGING

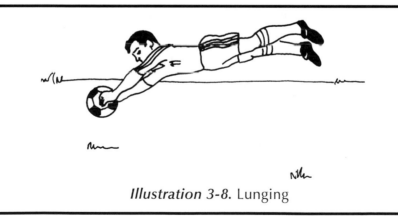

Illustration 3-8. Lunging

The Mechanics

Goalkeepers must learn to lunge for the ball. Most often, they must lunge out in front of the goal or on their sides against the ground. This drill is meant to teach confidence in lunging and reduce the fear of diving at the ball. This drill is intended to instruct goalkeepers to eventually fly through the air for a short distance and land on the cushioning ball: At first they must learn to dive for a short distance and use the ball as a cushion. *Note:* This drill can help reduce the novice goalkeeper's apprehension of diving through the air: With experience and confidence, mature goalkeepers will learn advanced techniques for diving across the goal mouth. After experience has been gained, the coach and player may investigate more advanced methods. More advanced training of this nature is beyond the scope of this text.

The lunge is shown in *Illustration 3-8* (see previous page). Prior to performing this drill, choose a place in a soft grassy area that has been inspected for anything injurious. With the area cleared of any glass, stones etc., the goalkeeper is ready for diving practice provided that he is wearing protective gear such as elbow and knee protectors and an athletic supporter with or without a cup.

During this drill, the goalkeeper will be leaping with outstretched hands, first onto the stationary ball then onto a moving ball. *Note:* Landing on the ball will absorb much of the impact but not all. At this point in time, with the ball grasped firmly with the hands, the goalkeeper is to bring it into the midsection and curl around it for protection.

A coach or assistant coach will have more success passing on a technique such as this one by practicing it before hand: It is advisable for the coach to practice this drill several times in private, prior to the student goalkeeper's training.

The Drill

Part 1 (Stationary Ball)

- Set up the drill area and goal as follows. Reference *Figure 3-4*. In the cleared grassy area of the field, place a field marker to represent the first upright goalpost (shown inside and at the top of the cleared area). Place another reference field marker at a location 10' (3m) below the first one: A full size goal is not necessary for this drill. The first field marker will be in the area of diving practice while the second one can be placed in any convenient location. These two field markers represent a goal. Place a soccer ball about 1' (.3 m) up field from the grassy area goalpost and 1' (.3m) over, towards the other field marker. The ball is now simulating a stopped motion as it is heading perpendicularly towards the goal.

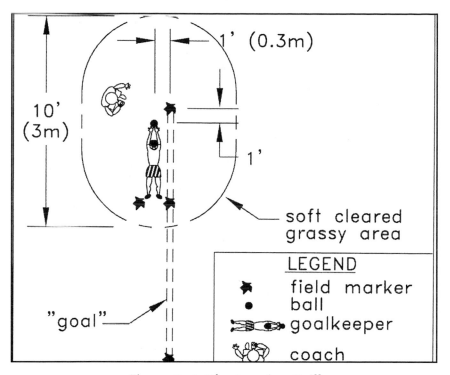

Figure 3-4. The Lunging Drill

- Have the goalkeeper lay face down on the ground (in the grassy area) and reach out to touch the ball with his finger tips. His feet are to be pointing in the direction of the other goalpost and he is to be lying parallel to the goal: This is a measurement to keep the goalkeeper separated from the ball by the length of his body with outstretched arms to the fingertips. Place a field marker at both sides of the goalkeeper's feet with the feet at the upper edges of the field markers.

- Have the goalkeeper stand up without moving his feet. He is now in a ready position (standing between the field markers at his feet) for the lunge at the ball.

- Jumping from the balls of his feet, the goalkeeper is to leap towards the ball and land hands first on it before his body contacts the ground.

- Just after contact with the ball, the goalkeeper is to curl up around the ball using the hands and body for ball protection. If the goalkeeper is timid and cannot reach the ball at its present location, move it closer until confidence is gained. Afterwards, place it back at its original location.

- After 12 successful lunges, rearrange the field markers so that the goalkeeper will be diving to his other side, i.e., rotate the lower goal field marker 180 degrees such that it is now 10' (3m) above the one in the grassy area. Then relocate the ball and perform the same measurement technique as explained in paragraph 2 above, but with the goalkeeper rotated 180 degrees from the original position, i.e., a mirror image from the ball is formed from the one shown in *Figure 3-4*.

- Repeat the practice with 12 more successful lunges.

- **The assistant coach is to observe that the goalkeeper lands on his hands before the body contacts the ground and that he curls around the ball.**

Part 2 (Rolling Ball)

The Drill

- This procedure is similar to the previous one except that the ball is actually rolling in a perpendicular direction towards the goal.

- The coach is to slowly roll the ball across the same spot as in the static case, and in the direction of the goal. At this point, the goalkeeper is to make a flying save.

- Perform this drill 12 times on each side of the goal.

- When the goalkeeper is successful with the slow rolling balls, repeat this exercise again 12 times with faster rolling balls on each side of the goal.

- **The coach is to make the same observations as explained in the last item in bulleted list above.**

3b. Goalkeeping Drills— Advanced

Drill 3.8

GOALKEEPING DEFENSE

The Mechanics

Now that the goalkeeper has learned the basic defending and attacking skills, and the field players have learned the Basic Backing-Up move, the players have the elements to put together a strong defensive team. This drill is intended to instill into the goalkeeper that he is not alone in defense of the goal. He must learn that he and the defensive persons integrate to form a cohesive defense team (or a cohesive attack team when the team has possession of the ball). Since the goalkeeper is facing upfield, he is in the best position to command other players to cover unmarked opponents.

This drill uses five players: a goalkeeper, two defenders and two attackers. Reference *Figure 3-5* (see page 79). The attacking players are even numbered and the defenders are odd numbered. An attack begins, as shown in **Stage 1**, with the first attacking player (Player #2) leaving the Attackers' Starting Position while dribbling the ball towards the goal. As the player with the ball (Player #2) approaches the field marker located at A, the defender near the goal (Player #1) runs up to approach him. At that point in time, Player #4, the attacker's assistant, leaves the line to catch up with him. When Player #4 reaches Location A, the goalkeeper is to summon the next defensive player in line (Player #3) to pick up the unmarked Player #4.

Now when Player #1 reaches Player #2 he places himself goal-side of the attacker and backs up with him in the same manner as performed in the Basic Backing-Up Defense Drill: He will now be controlling the motion of the dribbling attacker (Player #2). In the meantime, as shown in **Stage 2**, Player #3 (leaving the line) is accelerating to get into a position in front of the unmarked attacker (Player #4). Player #4 now is near to Player #2.

When Player #3 catches up with Player #4, he is to get goal-side of him for the remainder of the attack. The two attackers, now constrained, must attempt to score. Player #2 can take a shot at the goal or pass the ball to Player #4 for the shot.

If the shot is caught by the goalkeeper, he is then to call to one of his defenders (Players #1 or #3) to move back downfield into an open space to receive the ball; he then makes the throw quickly but calmly, maintaining proper form. As the ball arrives at the defender, he moves to it, stops and traps it. The second defender is to move nearby for a pass from the teammate. During this drill, the original attackers are not to interfere with the goalkeeper's passing or the other players' reception. The drill is completed when the second teammate traps the ball.

Notes

- If the above description seems too complicated to clearly understand, the procedure for the drill is repeated below, but somewhat differently.
- This drill is extremely important for the goalkeeper's defensive control as he helps control attacking players and starts off a new attack with a controlled pass to one of his teammates.

The Drill

- Set up the field as shown in *Figure 3-5*. The goal can be a regulation goal or constructed from two field markers.
- The goalkeeper is to be in the normal position 4' to 5' (1.2 m to 1.5 m) in front of the goal.
- At the signal from the coach, attacker (Player #2) starting at the attackers' field markers begins to dribble towards the goal, as shown in **Stage 1**.
- When Player #2 approaches Location A the defender (Player #1) stationed near the goal runs up to meet him.
- When Player #1 reaches Player #2 he positions himself goal-side of his attacker and backs up with him until he comes within 10' (3 m) of the goal at the field marker at Location B.
- In the meantime, when Player #2 reaches Location A, an attacking assistant (Player #4) runs from the line towards Player #2.

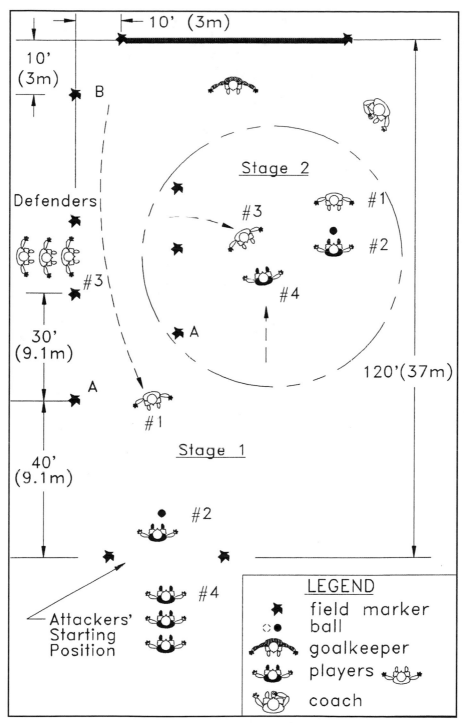

Figure 3-5. Goalkeeping Defensive Drill

- When he reaches Location A, the goalkeeper is to motion and call to the next defender on line to cover Player #4.
- Player #3 then runs to get goal-side of Player #4 as shown in **Stage 2**.
- Both attacking players are now under pressure and must make an effort to take a shot on goal.
- If the goalkeeper catches the ball, he is to signal to either defender that he means to pass the ball to him. He then throws a pass to that defender who in turn is then to pass it to the other defender without interference from the 2 attackers. If, on the other hand, a goal is scored or the ball is kicked over the goal line, the drill is finished.
- This concludes the attack and the players are to join the opposite lines. As their turn comes up for the second time in either offense or defense, have the players change positions, i.e., 4 becomes 2 and 1 becomes 3, etc.
- **The coach is to observe that the defenders back up and constrain their attackers and, most importantly for this drill, he is to observe that the goalkeeper is watching his defense and calling for a player (Player #3) to cover the open player (Player #4).**

Drill 3.9

GOALKEEPER CORNER KICK DEFENSE

The Mechanics

This drill is designed to instruct players (mostly defensive players) on their positioning for this defensive tactic against corner kicks. The goalkeeper should stand in either one of two positions, depending upon the age level of the goalkeeper's team.

Young goalkeepers should be located from the center of the goal to one-third of the distance from the far post. Reference *Figure 3-6A*. Place two players on each side of the goal. Position another defensive player on the far side of the goal, as shown, to mark any nearby attacker. Other defensive players (not shown) should mark any other attacking players while endeavoring to remain goal-side of their attacker.

More experienced goalkeepers should be positioned at one-third to one-half of the goal distance as measured from the near post as shown in

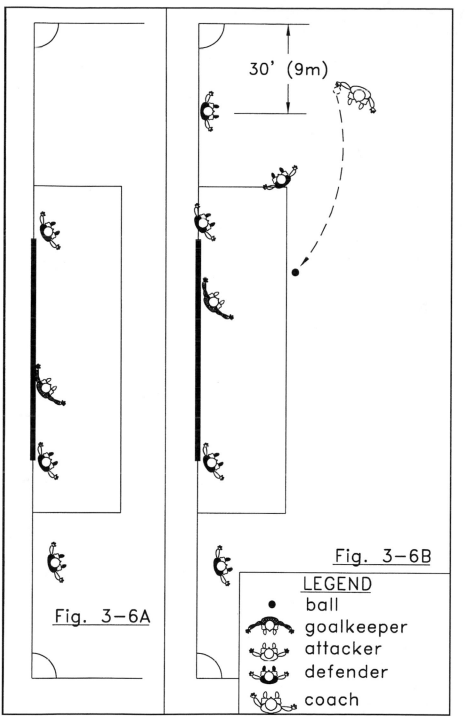

30' (9m)

Fig. 3—6B

Fig. 3—6A

LEGEND
● ball
goalkeeper
attacker
defender
coach

Figure 3-6. Goalkeeping Corner Kick Defense Drill

Figure 3-6B. Locate a defender within 30' (9 m) from the corner nearest the ball. Place a defense person at the far rear post and another just in front of the near post, as shown. Place another defense person on the far side of the goal, as shown, to mark any nearby attacker. Other defensive players (not shown) should mark an opponent but keep sufficient distance to assure that they will always remain goal-side of these players as they prepare and make their assault on the goal.

In all cases, two wing attackers (not shown and part of your defensive team) should be stationed up near the midfield line. This positioning puts them in a strategic location for a counter attack as the ball often gets re-located there after the corner kick.

This drill requires the use of a full defensive team along with the use of four offensive (attacking) players.

The Drill

- Locate the defensive players as shown in *Figure 3-6* (see previous page). Locate four attackers (not shown and part of the attacking team) about 50' (15 m) evenly spaced and in line, and back from, and parallel to the goal (the exact placement of the attackers will depend upon the players' age level and experience). They are to rush in as soon as the ball is thrown in front of the goal (no corner kicker is used).

- The coach should stand near the goal line, several feet in from the corner. The exact location will depend upon the coach's ability to throw the ball. *Note:* The ball is to be thrown to all locations where a possibility of scoring occurs. Throws are more accurate and efficient than kicks; and as a reminder, propelling the ball via a throw or kick produces the same effect.

- Practice these defensive corner kicks by throwing the ball into the defensive area such that it is out of range of the goalkeeper's hands.

- The attacking players are to attempt to score.

- The defensive players are to eject the ball safely out towards the wings, i.e., kick or head the ball out. The goalkeeper is to clear the ball out to any safe area using any method, if the ball cannot be caught safely. If the ball is caught, the goalkeeper is to start a counter attack with a throw to an open teammate. The opposition, in this drill, may try to intercept the ball.

- Run this drill for 15 minutes.

- **The coach is to observe that balls not caught are propelled safely up field and towards the wings by the goalkeeper and defensive players, that the defenders correctly mark attackers and that the defending team's wing players are in position for a possible counter attack. The ball may also be tipped over the goal.**

Drill 3.10
DEFENSE ON BREAKAWAYS

The Mechanics

Breakaway Defense

A breakaway is a term in soccer meaning that the goalkeeper is all alone with one or more opponents attacking his goal while the defense has been caught down field. This condition can be mostly avoided when the goalkeeper has total control of the defense. There will be times, however, when young and inexperienced goalkeepers are put into this position and need a set procedure to follow for the defense of the goal. Normally, the goalkeeper will be positioned in the center of the goal, but standing 4' to 5' to the front of it. When a breakaway by a single opponent occurs, the goalkeeper should make one of two choices: with proper timing, either run out to meet the attacker at 12 yards (11m) to grab the ball at the opponent's feet, or move out to a 12' (3.6 m) radius to meet this threat by just opposing the opponent dribbling the ball. Reference *Figure 3-7* (see page 84). If the second choice is made, it is then the choice of the attacker to attempt to dribble around the goalkeeper or chip the ball over his head.

The goalkeeper must be totally committed to his decision. Whatever is the choice, a balanced angle must be maintained: This means that if the attack is coming from the right or left side of the goal, the goalkeeper moves along the 12' (3.6 m) radius such that he protects both sides of the goal equally. There can be *no* hesitation on his part as he must totally commit himself to do whatever is his choice. Any hesitation will be sensed by the attacker and take the pressure off of him; but, a rapid advance by the goalkeeper will force the offender to make a quick pressured decision.

If the breakaway consists of two attackers, the method requires no thinking. The goalkeeper is to move to meet the attacker with the ball by moving to a goal-side position at the 12' (3.6 m) radius in front of the goal. He

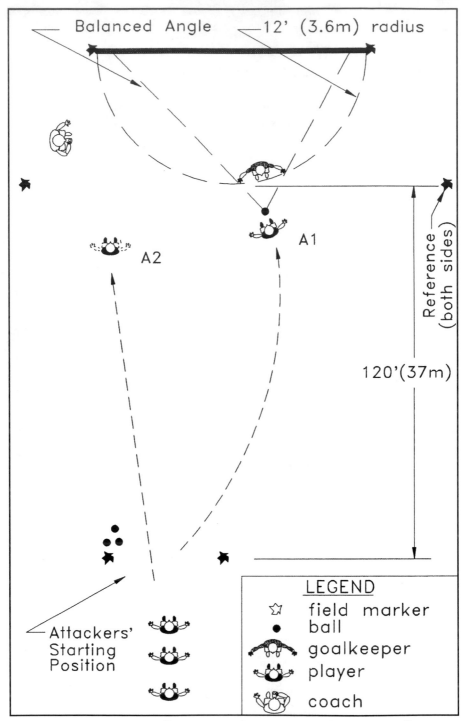

Figure 3-7. Goalkeeper Defense on Breakaways Drill

is to face the ball dribbling opponent with the angles balanced. If the ball is then passed to the second attacker, this is the time that the goalkeeper must make his next move. He must concentrate only on the second opponent and remain goal-side of him while keeping the angles balanced, i.e., the goalkeeper must completely forget about the other attacker and only concentrate on the opponent with the ball.

The Drill

- Set up the drill as shown in *Figure 3-7*.
- Player #1 is to leave the Attackers' Starting Position and to dribble the ball while Player #2 follows him and runs alongside of him, but slightly behind him.
- When Player #1 is confronted by the goalkeeper, he passes the ball to Player #2.
- The goalkeeper then confronts Player #2 and disregards Player #1.
- Player #2 then takes a shot at the goal.
- Regardless of the outcome, the drill is over.
- The players then return to the end of the line.
- When the attacking players' turns come up the second time, they are to play the reverse rolls.
- Run the drill for 15 minutes.
- **The coach is to observe that the goalkeeper confronts both players confidently and without hesitation as he quickly switches coverage from Player #1 to Player #2.**

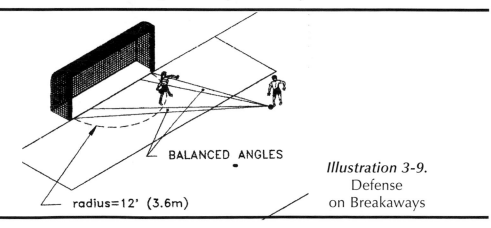

BALANCED ANGLES

radius=12' (3.6m)

Illustration 3-9.
Defense
on Breakaways

4. Intermediate Field Drills—Offensive

Drill 4.1

HIGH BALL INSIDE-OF-THE-FOOT TRAP

The Mechanics

Trapping high balls with the inside of the foot is accomplished by placing the body at a 90 degree angle to the path of the ball. The player then elevates his trapping leg such that the inside of the foot just meets the ball. The flight of the ball can be anywhere from lower chest height to nearly ground level. As the ball is contacted with the instep, it is cushioned by allowing the foot to recoil on impact. This move allows the ball to drop dead at the feet. It is to drop, not rise, as a rising action will take too much settling time causing the opposition players to possibly intercept the ball. The trapping process requires that the player keep his eyes on the ball during the entire procedure.

The drill is performed as follows: The coach is to throw the ball underhanded. To novice trappers, the throw is made rather slowly. As the players improve their trapping ability, the throws should be made more rapidly to reduce the dropping arc of the thrown ball.

Illustration 4-1. High Ball Inside-of-the-Foot Trap

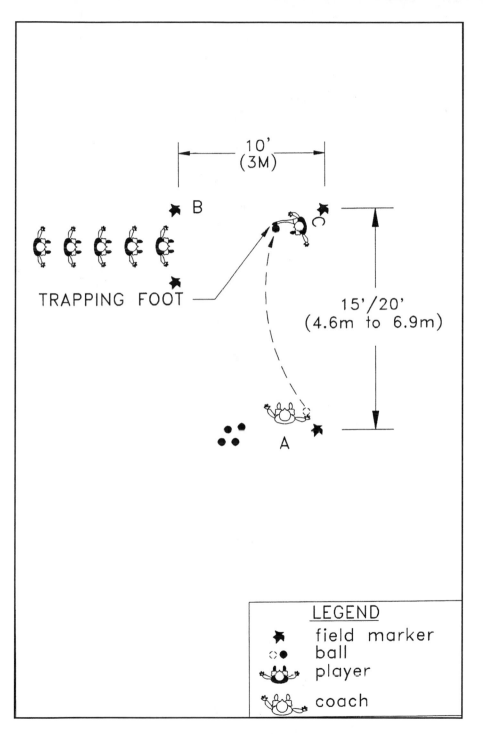

Figure 4-1. High Ball Inside-of-the-Foot Trap Drill

The Drill

- Set up the field as shown in *Figure 4-1* (see previous page). If there is an assistant coach, explain the aim of the drill and duplicate the drill setup. The coach stands at the field marker located at A and the first player on the line located at B moves to the field marker at Location C.

- The coach is to throw the ball underhanded. The first throws are to the right foot of the player at a point that the trapping player must lift his leg to meet the ball. In order to make this trap, the player must turn to his right approximately 90 degrees.

- Repeat the sequence such that each player gets to make four successful traps at different heights.

   The trapping player, while keeping his eyes on the ball, will trap the ball dead in order that it drops just below the trapping foot.

   After each player has had one turn of four successful traps, he is to go to the end of the line. At his next turn, he is to repeat this trapping exercise using the left foot and reversing the procedure of Step 2 above.

- Run the exercise with sufficient time to assure that each player has had at least two turns at trapping the ball with each foot.

- **The coach is to observe that the player keeps his eyes on the ball during the entire trapping procedure and that the ball drops downward immediately and dead just below the trapping foot.**

Drill 4.2

INTERMEDIATE DRIBBLING

The Mechanics

Intermediate dribbling is a homework drill designed for all field players and should be also practiced by the goalkeeper. It can be performed at home as well as in training in an area that is clean, free from debris and not slippery. Its purpose is to develop agility and improve the sense of balance. It is designed to force players to touch the ball with every dribbling step. *Illustration 4-2A* shows the lower portion of a player dribbling in a figure eight loop. This drill is designed to teach players to gain total control

4-2A   4-2B

Illustration 4-2. Intermediate Dribbling. *Illustration 4-2A* shows the path of the drill in the form of a figure eight and *Illustration 4-2B* shows a player making the sharp turn required for this drill.

of the ball while developing the sense of touch with the feet. In addition, players learn to turn sharply while dribbling, as shown in *Illustration 4-2B*. Every step is used to contact the ball with either the inside or the outside of the foot. The front of the foot is used to hook and turn the ball between 90 and 180 degrees just after crossing "x" of the figure eight.

This is a fast drill and tends to easily wind players. For this reason it is recommended that players start out with three 20-second drill periods and build up to three 1-minute periods. A great advantage of this drill, as with all homework drills, is that it can extend the training beyond practices. To ensure that players practice this drill at home, a weekly demonstration of their dribbling ability with this drill should be a requirement.

Drill

- **The coach or an advanced player must demonstrate this drill prior to implementation.**

- Place each player with a ball in a rectangular array 20' (6.1 m) apart as they will need space as to not interfere with one another. The players are to dribble the ball in a figure eight. *Each loop* of the figure eight is to be about 4 to 5' (1.2 to 1.5 m) in diameter, as shown in *Illustration 4-2A*.

- The players are to dribble with every step touching the ball by using the front inside of the foot and the front of the outside of the foot to guide the ball. It must also be remembered that the ball is pushed, not tapped, otherwise the player will not have control of it. *Note* the turn being made in *Illustration 4-2B* (see previous page): The player must lean in the direction of the turn. As he changes direction, his balance is shifted to his opposite side. As players become proficient, they are to increase their speed.

- The players are to initially perform this drill three times in practice for 20-second periods with a half-minute break in between.

- The players are then assigned this drill as homework to be performed twice during the week, for a total of ten minutes each in both sessions.

- **Each week, the drill is to be demonstrated using groups of four players at a time. These players are to perform in front of the team. The nonparticipating players (the spectators) are to pick the best one from each group. This player is the winner of the group. At the end of the full team drill review, the losers are to do one lap around the field. The results of the training will be obvious in scrimmage games.**

Drill 4.3
Intermediate Shielding

The Mechanics

This drill is the fourth of five shielding drills with increased opponent pressure during both the trapping and dribbling portions of this drill. The pressure, gradually introduced in the shielding drills 2.5, 2.7 and 2.11, is now combined. With this drill, nearly full game/opponent pressure is implemented. But, full pressure during the trapping phase is still not fully applied. Full game pressure is only applied during the fifth shielding drill: The Monkey in the Middle drill located in Chapter 6b, Advanced Field Drills—Defensive.

During this drill, the pressure exerted by the opponent *during trapping* will be such that it will be applied from the trapping player's rear only (in actual game situations, an opponent may apply pressure to a trapping player from any direction). The pressure (less then maximum during trapping) applied from the rear only, still allows the trapper some learning space. After the trapper/dribbler gets the ball under control, she is to dribble it back to a field marker and proceed in a similar manner as in Drill 2.6 (see *Figure 2-6* on page 40). Unlike previous shielding drills, during the dribbling phase of this drill, the opponent is permitted to apply full pressure and can encircle the dribbler from 360 degrees. The dribbler must now shield and protect the ball from the opponent who may come in from any possible direction as she dribbles the ball to and from each field marker, and back to the middle. Arriving at the middle of the field markers, after the third pass of the field markers, she is to make her final move with a pass to her teammate. The pass is a shielded one using the foot furthest from the opponent.

The Drill

- Set up the drill according to *Figure 2-6* (see page 40) using four players for each drill group. As in the other drills, the players in similar jerseys are on the same team. The field markers separate the players by 20' (6.1 m). The 15' (4.5 m) markers signify an imaginary line that constrains the players. The players with the light jerseys may only move along this line when dribbling and the players in the dark jerseys may now move anywhere while trying to remove the ball from their opponents; however, the players in the light jerseys will need to move forward of the line during the trapping process.

- During **Stage 1** and **Stage 2**, follow the movements of Group 1 in the figure. During **Stage 3**, follow the movements of Group 2.

- After the ball is kicked to a teammate, she (the player in the light jersey) is to move to the ball and make the trap (any trap can be made during this drill). This is **Stage 1**. During the trap, the trapper must keep her eyes on the ball. The opponent is to be at her rear and apply pressure during the trap, but cannot move to the right or left of the trapper.

- After the ball is under control by the trapping player, she is to dribble back to one of the field markers. During this time, **Stage 2**, the opponent is to apply pressure and continue to do so for the remainder of the drill, as the opponent is now free to move anywhere to apply this pressure.

- During **Stage 3**, the dribbler is to dribble the ball to one of the field markers, to the next one, back to the first one and then back towards the middle.

  While dribbling the ball to the field markers, the dribbling player must keep the ball screened from her opponent.

- After the player has dribbled the ball back to the middle, she is then to return the ball to her teammate with a brisk pass and the procedure starts over again with her teammate. The pass must be made by the opposite foot from the side where the opponent is situated.

- When the first two teammates have completed the exercise, the players are to switch roles, i.e., the dribbling players now become the defenders and vice versa.

- The duration of this drill should be 15 minutes.

- **For this drill, the coach is to observe that pressure from the opponent is to be applied only to the rear of the trapping player during the trap. During the dribbling portion, the dribbler is to maintain her body between the opponent and the ball while full pressure is applied by the opponent. If this does not occur, the drill is to be stopped and the purpose is to be re-explained to any or all players.**

- **The coach is to observe that the final pass made to the teammate is made such that it cannot be blocked by the opponent as it must be made with the foot most distant from the opponent.**

Drill 4.4
THE BODY TRAP

The Mechanics

This is a unique trap utilizing different rules than in other traps as it does not require the player to trap the ball near the body. This drill instructs players on a method for controlling a ball that is seemingly bouncing out of control while sought after by a member of both teams. To simulate this condition, the ball is thrown in front of the trapping player nearly vertically in the air, about 30 to 40' (9 to 12 m) high. With the ball bouncing, the player runs towards the ball and aligns himself with it. He is then to push it with any part of his body such as the knee, stomach etc. (with the exception of hand or arm), in some preferred direction where there is no opponent.

This drill initially uses the coach to apply only slight pressure to the trapping player for about the first two or three tries, to demonstrate to the team the proper amount of pressure to be exerted here: Too much pressure will not help the team to get the idea behind the nature of this trap. After the team gets the message, with the proper pressure from the coach, players from behind the line located at B are to relieve the coach from this duty and apply the opponent pressure for the upcoming traps as shown in *Figure 4.2*.

Illustration 4-3.
The Body Trap

The trapping player coming from Location A is to make the trap. This trapping player is to initially contact the ball and guide it in some direction up to 40' or 50' (12 to 15 m) from the point of initial contact. As the player body-pushes the ball as shown in *Illustration 4-3*, he is to slow it down while maneuvering it to get it under his control. He will have to steer it away from his opponent in the process. After the ball is under control, it is to be delivered back to the coach.

The Drill

- Set up the drill as shown in *Figure 4-2* (see next page).

- Throw the ball in front of the trapping player, located initially at A (**Stage 1**), such that it rises 30 to 40' (9 to 12m) and lands directly in front of him. As the ball descends, you (the coach) are to approach the site of the ball impacting the ground as if you are competing with the trapping player for the ball (**Stage 2**). Do this a few times for the first drill session, then utilize a player from the line located at B for subsequent traps.

- The trapping player is to move to the ball and align himself with the ball's motion as it bounces (**Stage 3**). He is then to body-push it in some preferred direction away from the competing player (the coach). The coach or the second player from behind the line at B

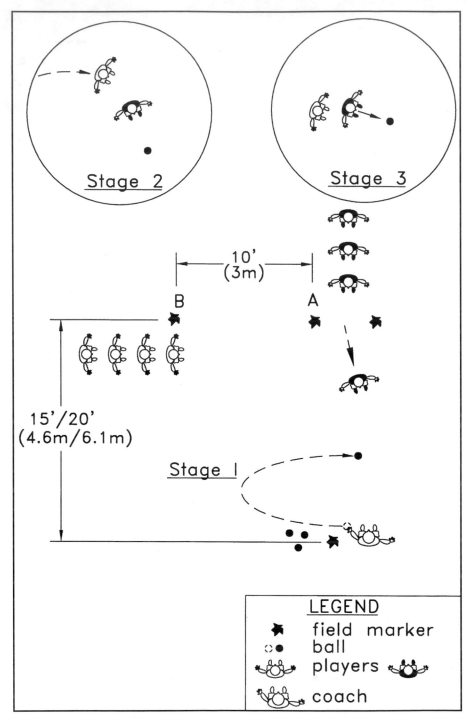

Stage 2

Stage 3

10'
(3m)

B

A

15'/20'
(4.6m/6.1m)

Stage 1

LEGEND
field marker
ball
players
coach

Figure 4-2. The Body Trap Drill

is to compcte for thc ball, but still allow the original trapping player to end up with it. With each successive day of this drill, the second player is to apply more pressure.

- As the ball slows down and comes under control, the player is to dribble it for several feet, then pass it back to the coach.

- **Observe that the trapping player aligns himself with the ball's moving direction just prior to contact and that he ends up controlling the ball at the end of the run (trap).**

Drill 4.5
The Outside-of-the-Foot Kick

The Mechanics

This drill is performed in the same manner as the Instep Kick in Drill 2.1 (see page 19). This kick, however, is made with the right foot when the ball is on the left side of the body and vice versa for the right side of the

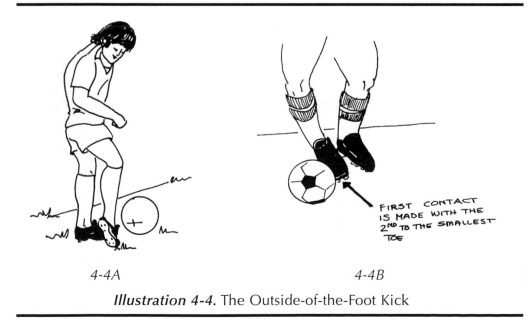

4-4A   4-4B

Illustration 4-4. The Outside-of-the-Foot Kick

body. This kick produces a spin that causes a curved flight path in opposition to the curvature of the Angled Instep Kick: When the kick is made with the right foot, the spin causes the ball to bend towards the right side of the kicker. The kicking motion prior to the kick is shown in *Illustration 4-4A* (see previous page). The kick is performed in the following manner: For a right-footed kick, the ball is just to the left side of the body midline. Place the nonkicking foot (the toes) at the rear of the ball about 6 to 12 inches (15 to 30 cm). The ball is then struck with the part of the foot containing the three smaller toes, as shown in *Illustration 4-4B* (see previous page). The knee is straightened out during the kick and the power then comes from the thigh. The kick must be made by keeping the eyes on the ball during the kick and during the follow through.

Variation for Kicking Around a Wall

When the players develop the skill to make this kick as described above, this variation may be substituted for the static situation of Drill 2.1 (see page 21): This variation enables the kicker to kick the ball around a wall of players (by a curved flight path) and into the goal. The goal would be guarded by this wall when the opposing team is penalized for some infraction. To use this kick for bending the flight of the ball around a wall (while keeping it relatively low), it is preferable to place the nonkicking foot near to the ball (to the left side of the ball for a right-footed kick). The first ball-contact will then be made by the second smallest toe. The kicker's aim should be 3 to 5' (1 to 1.5 m) to the left side of the wall to just clear the wall and compensate for the curved flight of the ball. The wall is normally placed at 10 yards (9.15 m) from the ball.

The Drill

- The drill is set up and run in the same manner as shown in Drill 2.1, The Basic Instep Kick Drill and using *Figure 2-1* (see page 21).

- Follow the identical procedures (Version 1 and Version 2) as described in Drill 2.1, except utilize the specialized kicking information in the Mechanics section of this drill. *Note:* as mentioned above when the players become proficient in making this kick, Version 1 of Drill 2.1 may be used to kick "around the wall" described in Drill 5.6 (see page 128).

- **The coach is to observe that the ball is struck with the lower part of the foot (the bottom three toes) and that the kicker keeps his eyes on the ball during the kick and during the follow through.**

Drill 4.6
JUMP AND BOUNCE

The Mechanics

The Jump and Bounce drill is the second homework drill designed for all field players, including the goalkeeper. Assign this drill a minimum of three weeks after assigning Intermediate Dribbling, homework Drill 4.2. This drill can be performed at home as well as in training in an area that is clean, free from debris and not slippery. Its purpose is to develop the sense of touch for better ball handling and dribbling. Each player is to bring their soc-

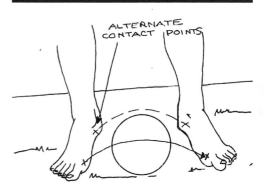

Illustration 4-5. Jump and Bounce

cer ball to practice for the purpose of demonstrating their skill before the coach and team by kicking the ball back and forth between the feet as they jump up. The ball is to bounce between the points of the foot as shown in *Illustration 4-5*. The principal points are in the front part of the foot, but the alternate points are more rearward and should be utilized part of the time that the drill is performed.

This drill is designed to force players to touch the ball with every dribbling step. The illustration shows a player's feet and the points of contact for the ball. This drill teaches players to gain more sensitivity by increasing the sense of touch with the feet. Every jump is used to contact the ball with the inside of either foot.

This is a fast drill and tends to easily wind players. For this reason it is recommended that players start out with three 20-second drill periods and build up to three 1-minute drills at home. The advantage of all homework drills is that they can extend the training beyond practices. To assure that players practice this drill at home, a weekly demonstration of their dribbling ability with this drill should be a requirement.

The Drill

- **The coach or an advanced player must demonstrate this drill prior to implementation.**

- Place each player with a ball in a rectangular array 10' (3 m) apart.

- They are to bounce the ball between the feet with every jump. As they jump, they are to touch the ball by using the front of the foot or the front of the rearward portion of the foot to guide the ball. As players become proficient, they are to increase their speed.

- The players are to initially perform this drill three times in practice for 20-second periods with about a half-minute break.

- The players are then assigned this drill as homework to be performed twice during the week, for a total of ten minutes each in both sessions.

- **Each week, the drill is to be demonstrated (replacing the previous homework demonstration—Intermediate Dribbling) using groups of four players at a time: The previous homework drill is to be continued however. These players are to perform in front of the team. As in the previous homework drill, the non-participating players (the spectators) are to pick the best one from each group: This player is the winner of the group. At the end of the drill review, the losers are to do one lap around the field. The results of the training will be obvious in scrimmage games.**

Drill 4.7

THE DUCK BILL KICK

The Mechanics

This drill is performed in the same manner as the Instep Kick in Drill 2.1 (see page 19) and the Outside-of-the-Foot Kick in Drill 4.5 (see page 95). This kick is made with the right or left foot when the ball is near the midline of the body. It is made with the flat portion of the foot just above the toes, like a tennis ball being struck with the upper frontal part of a duck bill: thus its name is the Duck Bill Kick. This kick generally produces no spin nor causes a curved flight path, unless the ball is caught off to its side. It is performed in a similar manner as the Basic Instep Kick where the non-kicking foot is placed alongside of the ball; however, the contact is made with the toes instead of the laces of the soccer shoe.

The kicking motion prior to the kick is shown in *Illustration 2-1A*. The kick is performed in the following manner: For a right-footed kick, the ball is about in the center of the body midline. Place the toes of the nonkicking foot at the front of the ball to keep the shot low. To elevate the kick, the nonkicking foot is placed more towards the midline of the ball as it intersects the earth. The ball is then struck with the part of the foot connecting the three smaller toes, with the toes and ankle pointing downwards. The only difference between this and the Instep Kick (for small feet) is that the ball is struck lower on the foot and presents no difficulty for a kicker with large feet. The knee is straightened out during the kick and the power then comes from the thigh. The kick must be made by keeping the eyes on the ball during the kick and during the follow through.

The Drill

- The drill is set up and run in the same manner as shown in Drill 2.1, The Basic Instep Kick Drill and using *Figure 2-1* (see page 19).

- Follow the identical procedures as described in Drill 2.1, except utilize the information in the Mechanics section of this drill.

- **The coach is to observe that the ball is struck with the lower center part of the foot (the portion of the foot above the toes, mainly above the smaller three toes) and that the kicker keeps his eyes on the ball during the kick and during the follow through.**

Drill 4.8

STATIONARY ROLLING BALL

The Mechanics

The Stationary Rolling Ball drill is the third homework drill designed for all field players. There should be a period of three weeks before

Illustration 4-6.
Stationary Rolling Ball

assigning this drill after assigning the Jump and Bounce homework drill. It can be performed at home as well as in training in an area that is clean, free from debris and not slippery. Its purpose is to develop the sense of touch for better ball handling and dribbling. During the practice exercise, each player is to have a ball. They are to roll the ball around in a figure eight as they remain in a stationary position. This exercise is especially useful for indoor soccer.

The ball is to roll under all parts of the foot as shown in *Illustration 4-6*. The bottom of the foot will make contact with the ball while it rolls beneath it as the player makes a small figure eight.

This drill is designed to give players a feel for the ball while not looking at it. It also improves their sense of balance. The first few times the player is permitted to look at the ball to get the feel and action of the ball, but he must eventually perform this drill while looking elsewhere.

At practice, they should do three repetitions of this drill for a minimum of one minute for each foot, using both feet. As stated above, the advantage of homework drills is that they can extend the training beyond practices. To ensure that players practice this drill at home, a weekly demonstration of their dribbling ability with this drill should be a requirement.

The Drill

- **The coach or an advanced player must demonstrate this drill prior to implementation.**

- Place each player with a ball in a rectangular array 5' (1.5 m) apart. The players are to roll the ball in a figure eight for one minute.

- They are to switch feet and repeat the exercise for another minute. Do this three times with about 30 seconds between each repetition. As players become proficient, they are to increase their speed. Eventually, they are to be told that they cannot look down at the ball during the drill.

- The players are to be instructed to perform this drill three times at home during the week, for 2-minute periods with each foot.

- **Each week, the drill is to be demonstrated using groups of four players at a time. These players are to perform in front of the team. The non-participating players (the spectators) are to pick the best one from each group. This player is the winner of the group. At the end of the drill review, the losers are to do one lap around the field. The results of the training will be obvious in scrimmage games.**

Drill 4.9
SLIDING TACKLE

The Mechanics

The Sliding Tackle is a tactic used to remove the ball from a dribbling opponent. When performed correctly, it can be very effective, *but it must not be used by any defender when there is no goal-side teammate that can mark a dribbling opponent if the tackle is missed*. This is especially important near your own defending goal.

This technique is practically identical to the hook slide in baseball and is performed as follows: While an attacking opponent is dribbling, a defending player (your player) approaches the opponent from a near perpendicular direction, and while running at the opponent, slides into

Illustration 4-7. Sliding Tackle

the ball with one foot towards the center of the ball. The toe of this foot is then thrust to dislodge it. When slide tackling with the right foot, as shown in *Illustration 4-7,* the calves will cross each other while the left leg is bent at the knee by about 70 to 90 degrees. The fall is broken by landing on the lower hand (the left hand), then onto the left forearm. The ball must be kicked firmly with a thrust of the leg and foot. Reverse the procedure for a left-footed tackle.

The purpose of the tackle is to kick the ball out from under the dribbling opponent with the hope that it ends up with your own teammate or to slow down an attack by possibly kicking the ball over the touch line. While making the tackle, the tackling player is to go for the ball while being careful not to contact the dribbler. If the ball is successfully tackled, the dribbler must then avoid the leg of the tackler. This tactic should be only employed in the two-thirds of the field above your defending goal: Slide tackling in the one-third sector of your defense is a very risky move, where the backing-up defensive technique is a much safer method for preventing a goal.

The Drill

- Set up the field as shown in *Figure 4-3*.
- During **Stage 1** of the drill, the dribbling player at location C is to dribble in a straight line towards the goal located at A.
- During **Stage 2** the tackling player located at B (while timing the run) rushes at the dribbler to meet the player and the ball about midway (location D) between the starting position C and the goal A.
- In **Stage 3** the tackler is to slide tackle the ball from the dribbler.
- If the slide tackle is successful, the tackling player and the dribbler go to the end of the opposite lines that they emerged from. The tackling player is to retrieve the ball.
- If the slide is missed, the dribbler may take a shot on the goal.
- **The coach is to observe that the tackler slides into the ball and uses enough force to dislodge the ball completely from the dribbler.**

Drill 4.10

INTERMEDIATE BACKING-UP DEFENSE TACTIC

The Mechanics

The purpose of this drill is to instruct the defensive players on how to work with the goalkeeper on team defensive coordination and strategy. The

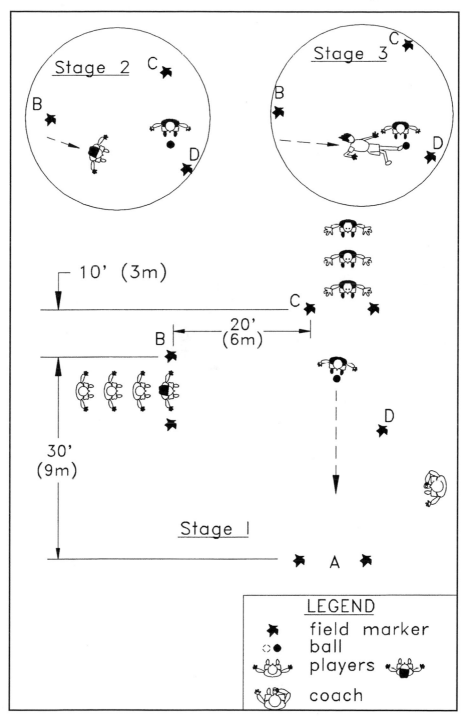

Figure 4-3. The Sliding Tackle Drill

defending players are to back up with their opponents as taught in Drill 2.10, the Basic Backing-Up Defense Drill.

The goalkeeper, having full view of the field at all times, must learn to protect himself with a second line of defense: The goalkeeper himself is the first line of defense. After having developed some of the elementary skills of deflecting and catching, he must now concentrate on his defenders. They must be aware that they are not to abandon him at any time by being caught too far up field. The goalkeeper must also assure that his defenders, under no circumstances, make the cardinal defensive mistake and attack the ball while it is under the control of the dribbling opponent. If, and only if, the dribbler loses the control of the ball and it is certain that the ball can be safely taken, then and only then may the defender do so. If the defender commits this error (regardless of the outcome), the goalkeeper is to be instructed to chastise the defender for doing so. The goalkeeper is also to command any other player to pick up any unmarked opponent.

This drill involves the employment of two attackers, two defenders and the goalkeeper. Two attackers (one with the ball) start an attack on goal. They are to be challenged by two defending players that position themselves in front of the attackers and back up with them while continually remaining goal-side of their opponents. They are to hold their ground and allow the attackers to make their moves when they have backed up to a certain point on the field. The attackers may pass the ball or take a shot on goal whenever they desire to do so.

The Drill

- Set up the drill according to *Figure 4-4* (see next page).

- At the start of the drill, the first attacker begins by dribbling the ball towards the goal as shown in *Phase 1*. The second attacker (on the line behind the player with the ball) moves to either side of the dribbler with the expectation of receiving a pass as shown in *Phase 2*. The second attacker must not become offside in the process. Concurrently with the attack commencement, the first two defenders in line each run to pick up an opponent. They then back up with their opponent until they reach the field marker set at 10' (3 m) from the goal.

- The dribbler may pass the ball or take a shot on goal.

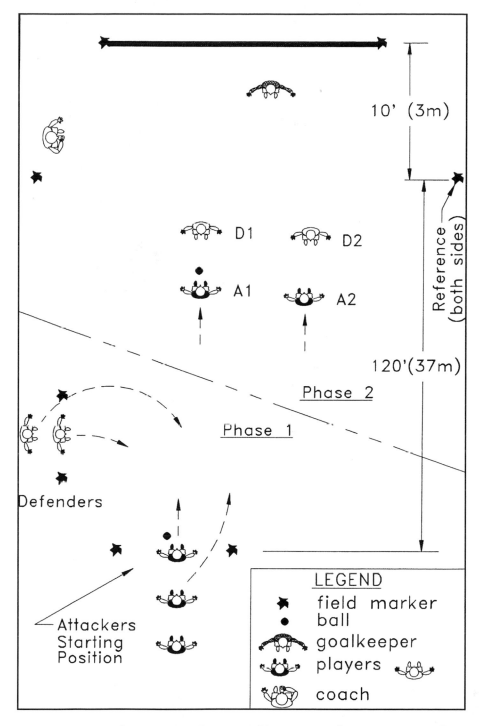

Figure 4-4. The Intermediate Backing-Up Defense Tactic Drill

- The goalkeeper is to oversee the defense and command his defense to do whatever is necessary to ensure that he is protected at all times with his second line of defense.

- **The coach is to determine that the goalkeeper understands his defensive roll. The coach must also insist that the defenders respond to the goalkeeper and not attack the ball while it is under control of the dribbling opponent. The coach is also to observe that the attacker without the ball does not go offside.**

Drill 4.11
SHOULDER CHARGE TACKLE

The Mechanics

The Shoulder Charge Tackle drill is an extremely beneficial drill to help develop the proper amount of legal soccer aggression. By legal, it is meant that it is permitted by the soccer International Laws of the Game. A player is permitted to have physical contact with an opponent if she is fairly charging this opponent when this opponent is dribbling the ball. The shoulder charge is the physical contact that one makes with an opponent when the tackler's shoulder comes into contact with the dribbler's shoulder for the purpose of nudging the opponent away from the ball in order to gain its possession. See *Illustration 4-8*. Note, illegal aggression related to this tactic is discussed below in the Drill section.

The purpose of this drill is two-fold:

Illustration 4-8.
Shoulder Charge Tackle

- To teach players the shoulder charging tackle to obtain possession of the ball.

- To teach players the amount of roughness allowed in the game and to create competitiveness in players that are normally intimidated by the overly aggressive behavior of some players.

This is an intense drill and should only be taught to children with the consent of their parents or guardians. The drill is performed in the following way: Referring to *Figure 4-5* (see next page), the coach throws the ball out in front of two players at the starting position, located at A, for the purpose of one player taking its possession. The player gaining the possession dribbles the ball towards the farthest field marker located at B. The player without the ball is to shoulder charge the dribbler with the purpose of dislodging the ball from the dribbler by making shoulder to shoulder contact. At the point where the new player has possession, the original player re-starts the process to regain ball possession. The drill should be performed such that both players gain possession of the ball at least two times during each drill, i.e., each player is to be the dribbler at least one time while heading for the farthest field marker at B or when returning back to A.

It must be pointed out that two misunderstandings generally occur during this drill; however, with the proper explanations, the players eventually get to understand the purpose of the drill. They are:

- The dominant player usually takes ball possession and does not allow the other player to gain its possession. This is alleviated (generally, during the drill play must be stopped for incorrect implementation by the players) by instructing the players that the drill is not a contest to determine who can keep the ball, but one where both players must exchange ball possession.

- Players tend to dribble in zig-zag patterns to protect the ball from getting stolen. While this is perfectly acceptable in games, it is not acceptable in this drill. The players are to be instructed to dribble only in a straight line to the distant field markers and allow the opponent to shoulder charge and win possession of the ball. Again, usually the drill must be stopped and the players given a further explanation on the proper requirements for this drill.

Note: After this drill has been performed properly at a few practices, you should see a marked improvement with your players winning the loose ball (competition to gain the ball's possession as it bounces or rolls along the ground).

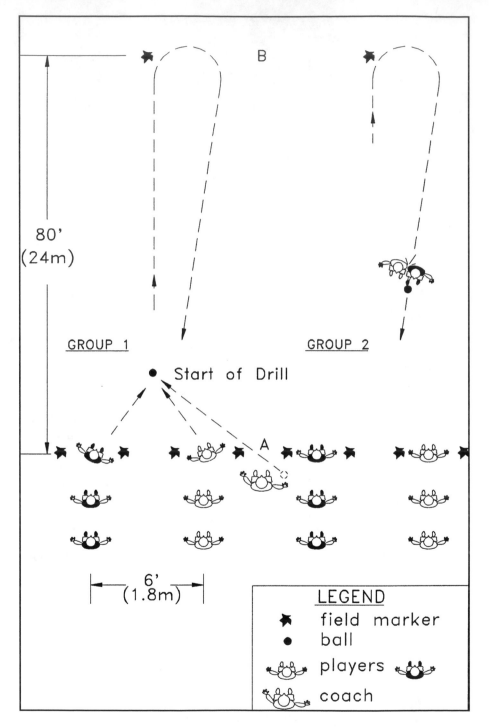

Figure 4-5. Shoulder Charge Tackle Drill

The Drill

- Set up the drill as shown in *Figure 4-5*. The explanation of the figure is as follows: The two players at the head of the lines of players on the left side of the field (Group 1) are about to start their drill as the coach throws out the ball. The two players on the right side of the field (Group 2) are shown with the drill in progress and nearly completing the drill: At this instant, the player in the dark jersey has possession of the ball and the player in the light jersey is shoulder charging.

- Two Group 1 players (standing at location A) are about to charge at the ball for the purpose of winning the loose ball after it has been thrown approximately 10' (3 m) in front of them.

- The player gaining its possession is to dribble the ball towards the field marker at Location B.

- The other player is to shoulder charge the opponent and thereby take possession of the ball at least one time during each trip.

- **Stop the drill and explain the drill:**

    If the ball is not being exchanged at least one time each as the players are racing towards the field markers located at B and A.

    If the players do not understand that the concept of the drill is to give each player a chance to make good shoulder charge tackles.

    If the dribbling player zig-zags.

- At the completion of the drill, each player is to join the rear of the next line by a clockwise, rotation.

- Run this drill for 15 minutes.

- **The coach is to observe that the players are making contact with the shoulders only. It is illegal to charge a player from behind, use any excessive roughness or to use any part of the body to contact the other player except with the shoulder. This information must be part of the instruction given each time prior to performing this drill.**

5a. Mid-Advanced Drills— Intermediate Offensive

Drill 5.1

TURNING WHILE DRIBBLING

The Mechanics

Turning sharply with the ball by 90 to 180 degrees very often results in a player losing it to the opposition: This is a poor practice. Obviously, turning blindly when it is certain that there is no opponent nearby is an acceptable practice. Most often, however, this is not the case and it is much safer to turn according to the procedure outlined in this drill. This drill is designed to instruct players how to turn safely with an opponent to their rear, i.e., it prepares a player to make a safe U turn.

The methodology behind this drill is to utilize the application of shielding to gradually turn in the opposite direction of the opponent's location. To accomplish this, the dribbling player is to keep her eye on the opponent with peripheral vision or watch her shadow while shielding and maneuvering the ball and herself into position to head up field. This is done by turning in the direction that the opponent is not guarding. When this is not possible, however, it is a good practice to pass the ball back to any unguarded teammate.

This drill begins with the dark jersey player located at B ready to move into position in front of location A. Reference *Figure 5-1.* The goalkeeper

Illustration 5-1.
Turning While Dribbling

110

then throws the ball to this player's feet. As the ball is thrown, the opponent located at the head of line C immediately rushes to the back of the trapper. The trapper moves to the ball and makes the trap. This is **Stage 1**. The trapper should arrive there a bit sooner than the opponent and have no difficulty shielding the ball immediately after trapping it; however, the distance may need to be adjusted one way or the other, depending upon the players' age and skill level. After getting the ball under control in **Stage 2**, the trapper is to begin turning by keeping a watch on the opponent with her peripheral vision or the opponent's shadow.

Illustration 5-1 shows the dribbler hooking her foot around the ball as she gradually makes the shielded turn. This is **Stage 3**. *Note 1:* The girl making the turn is balancing herself and not pushing off the opponent: Keeping one's arms up with the intent of warding off the opponent would be considered obstruction.

The turn should be made by moving in the direction of the closest touch line, if possible, making a gradual arc with approximately a 10' (3 m) radius. *Note 2:* Turns near your own defending goal should always be made in the direction of the touch line, since a mistake in front of your defending goal can cause an opponent to take possession of the ball. Near the touch line the dribbling player may reverse the turn direction if the original turn direction is blocked.

Note 3: It is very important for the coach to not accept a successful turn if made blindly; it invalidates the drill's requirements and must be discouraged. This move, if not checked, will frequently cause your team to lose the ball in games where the competition is strong.

The Drill

- Set up the drill as shown in *Figure 5-1* (see next page).

- The goalkeeper is to rapidly roll the ball to the feet of the player arriving from B when he reaches location A.

- This player then runs to the ball and makes the trap. Concurrently, as the ball is thrown, a player located at C runs up and applies pressure by attempting to dislodge the ball from the trapping player (dribbler). Depending on the skill level and age of the players, the distance from C to A may have to be adjusted to permit the player originally located at C to arrive just after the trap is being made. This is **Stage 1**.

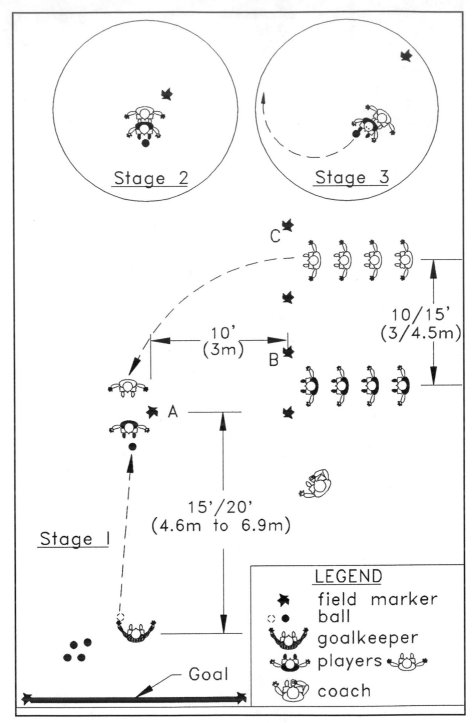

Stage 2

Stage 3

C

10/15'
(3/4.5m)

10'
(3m)

B

A

15'/20'
(4.6m to 6.9m)

Stage 1

Goal

LEGEND
✹ field marker
⊙ ● ball
🎽 goalkeeper
🧍 players 🧍
🧍 coach

Figure 5-1. The Turning While Dribbling Drill

- This player, after making the trap, dribbles a few feet towards the goalkeeper to get her balance and control of the ball as shown in **Stage 2**. She then turns slightly to locate the opponent. After locating the side that the opponent is favoring, she commences to make the turn in the opponent's opposite direction while shielding the ball. By keeping the opponent at bay, while screening her from the ball, the dribbler gradually turns towards the direction of her opponent's goal, as shown in **Stage 3**. *Note:* The dribbling player may choose to turn in any direction in this drill and at any time reverse the direction of the turn.

- This completes the drill. After the dribbler returns the ball to the goalkeeper both players join the rear of the opposite lines from which they emerged.

- Each player should have two turns at turning.

- **The coach is to observe that the ball is well shielded during the turn. Even if a blind turn has been successful it was done incorrectly and indicates that the dribbler was not following instructions. The exercise is to be repeated until the turn is made in the acceptable manner according to the drill procedure.**

Drill 5.2
THE TOP-OF-THE-THIGH TRAP

The Mechanics

The thigh trap is a useful trap for trapping balls arriving in the air at a level about midbody height while a player is facing the plane of the trajectory. The trapping method is as follows: A ball lobbed underhanded is sent to the player, with a rather sharp descent. See *Illustration 5-2* (on page 114). The player is to align himself with the plane of the trajectory and estimate the point of descent where the thigh will make contact with the ball. The player then lifts his thigh to a point that is parallel to the ground while the knee is relaxed and bent 90 degrees. As the ball drops, the player, with his eyes on the ball, allows the ball to contact the center point of the thigh. This is important as any other location will cause the ball to bounce into an uncontrollable position. As the ball makes contact, the leg is to recoil on impact to decrease the ball's rebound-ing elevation. As the ball drops, the player is to get control of the ball immediately, and dribble the ball about 10' (3 m).

The Drill

- Set up the drill according to *Figure 5-2*. If an assistant coach is available, give him an adequate explanation on what is to be expected from the drill and run the drills simultaneously.

- The player located at B moves to Location C. The coach, located at A, is to throw the ball in an arched fashion to the front of the player. The flight of the ball, as thrown at the trapper, has a flight path numbered #1 to #2. The ball should descend at #3 on the player's thigh and at a point where the player can easily trap it. **The 2:1 view should help in visualizing this set of movements.**

- The ball will then bounce slightly above the thigh and fall to the ground at position #4. At this point the trapper is to get control of the ball with the feet and dribble it for a few feet (about a meter).

- The player is to make three good traps with the right thigh. If the throws or traps are made badly, repeat the exercise until three good traps are made.

- The player then goes to the end of the line and is to repeat the exercise with the left thigh.

- Run the drill for 15 minutes.

- **The coach is to observe that the player keeps his eyes on the ball at all times and that the ball only bounces slightly in the vertical direction.**

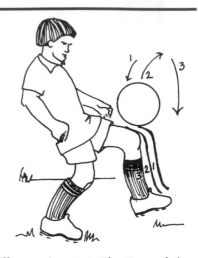

Illustration 5-2. The Top-of-the-Thigh Trap. The arrows and numbers indicate the time sequence for the movement of the ball and leg: (No. 1) the ball impacts the thigh as it rises to meet it. (No. 2) the ball rises slightly as the leg recoils downwards. (No. 3) the ball descends and lands just in front of the trapper as the leg is retracted to the ground.

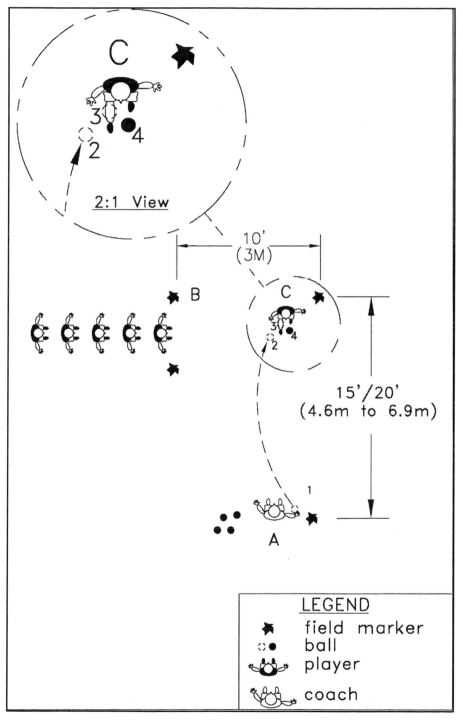

C

2:1 View

10'
(3M)

B

C

3
4
2

15'/20'
(4.6m to 6.9m)

1

A

Figure 5-2. The Top-of-the-Thigh Trap Drill

Drill 5.3
THE BLIND CROSS

The Mechanics

The Blind Cross, the most common cross-pass in soccer, is generally made to hopefully reach the head (or sometimes the foot) of an anticipating teammate in front of the opponent's goal, away from the goalkeeper's range. It is kicked from the corner area of the field to a teammate that is more or less in the center of the field, but usually located (field-wise) behind the kicker. The kicker must pull the ball backwards as he and the ball are moving forward rapidly, while normally being chased by an opponent. *Illustration 5-3* shows an idealized situation and location of players for the correctly made Blind Cross.

The Blind Cross is made with the right foot of a player dribbling along the right touch line and with the left foot while dribbling along the left touch line. The name "blind" comes from the fact that the player making the cross, in the fashion described above, has his vision generally obscured from the targeted receiver. The cross from the right side of the field and right foot is made as follows (naturally the situation is reversed on the left side of the field). A dribbling player (usually a wing player) races up the right side of the field near the touch line with an opponent at his heels. Generally, the dribbler, being restricted from curving herself inwards towards the middle of the field because of opponent resistance, dribbles nearly up to the goal line (near the corner) and then makes the cross to a particular teammate or just to any hoped for teammate.

For various reasons, amateurs almost always try to get as close to the goal line as possible before making the cross. In the most usual case, the ball is then blocked or tackled and the play is thwarted. If the dribbler does remain with the ball to the touch line, she has run out of space. She would then endeavor to kick the ball into the goal area while trying to pull it back far enough to be just out of range of the goalkeeper. This means that the ball must actually be pulled back about 10 or 15' (3 or 4.5 m) from its forward direction. This is not easy to do and is often a failed effort.

The cross is difficult to make for the following reasoning (and physics). Using the analogy of a clock laying flat on the field to describe the ball's direction, the ball would be heading at 12:00 as it is dribbled towards the goal line. The untrained player will generally kick the ball (from the right wing) at a point on the ball approximately at 3:00. Because of the ball's

Illustration 5-3. An Idealized Blind Cross

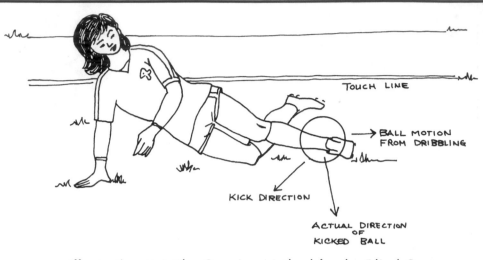

Illustration 5-4. The Crossing Method for the Blind Cross

forward motion, kicking it at 3:00 will cause the ball either to end up in a direction of at best 10:00, but usually ending up heading in the 11:00 direction and directly to the goalkeeper.

In order for a player to pull the ball back, out of the goalkeeper's range, she must hook her foot in front of the ball to make ball contact at about 1:30 to 2:00. Refer to *Illustration 5-4.* If this is not difficult enough, the problem is further aggravated by the need to keep the flight of the ball relatively low. Therefore, in addition to the forward contact, the ball must be hit at about its midline, parallel to the field. Experienced players can do this while remaining on their feet, but amateurs generally send the ball upwards with too much of an arc. As one may visualize, a properly executed blind cross is a difficult feat to accomplish. It is recommended that younger players make the kick by getting down on one hand as shown in *Illustration 5-4.* This will at least keep the flight of the ball low, providing that it is contacted at its midplane parallel to the ground.

In summary, the two aspects of making this kick properly, as previously discussed, are to hit the ball at 1:30 or 2:00 (depending upon the ball's location and forward speed), and at its midplane, parallel to the ground. It is also important that players are reminded to kick well before the last possible second before arriving at the touch line.

In professional soccer this play has a low success rate but it is effective enough to be used quite frequently; however, the lower the age level in the amateur ranks one goes, the less likely it is that one will observe a

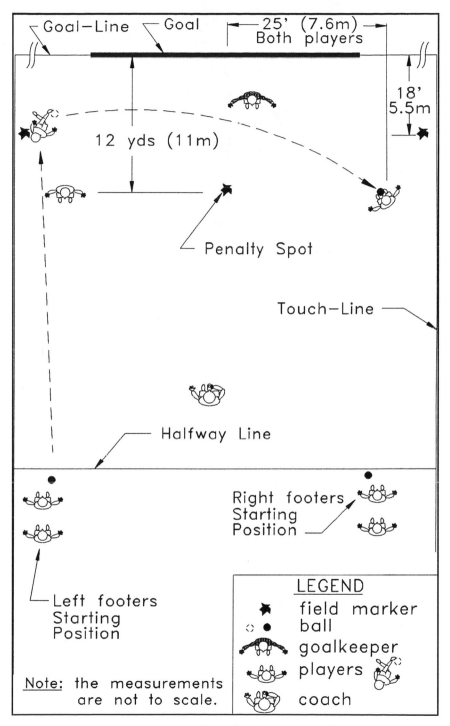

Figure 5-3. The Blind Cross Drill

successful cross. Young age group players seldom are successful in making a good cross, but young players should be exposed to the proper techniques if they are to become successful at it. Because of this, you, the coach, or an experienced player must not only realize this but be able to demonstrate this cross pass by dribbling along the touch line and dropping down on one hand just prior to the kick, and make a successful cross.

The Drill

- Each player should practice the positioning of the body prior to the actual drill.

- Set up the drill as shown in *Figure 5-3* (see previous page). Post two teammates down in front of the goal, as shown, along with a goalkeeper. Defending opponents are not used in this drill.

- The two lines at the Halfway Line are formed such that the right-footed kickers are on the right side and left-footed kickers are on the left-hand side of the field.

- The first player from one line is then to dribble the ball down the touch line. As she nears the goal line, she is to make the cross to the furthest teammate standing at a distance of the penalty spot to the side of the goal [12 yards (11 m)]. The left-footed cross will go to the teammate on the right side of the field. Young players should dribble the ball (along the wing) midway between the penalty spot and the touch line on their chosen side. In other words, they should not be too near the touch line. When the crosser reaches her destination (the place to execute the cross is roughly indicated by the field marker locations on the edge of the field), she is to kick the ball to the head of the player standing at the opposite side of the field. Adjust the receiving players' distance according to the age and skill level of the team.

- After the cross play, the kicker is to retrieve the ball and relieve the player on the other side of the penalty spot (the receiver). The player leaving this location is to join a line on his chosen side of the field.

- Alternate the lines of players as much as possible, yet each player should have the same amount of turns making the cross play.

- **The coach is to observe that the ball is pulled back away from the goalkeeper and that the elevation of the kick is at a reasonably** low arc. He should also observe that the player looks at the ball during the kick.

Drill 5.4
THE NON-BLIND CROSS

The Mechanics

The Non-Blind Cross serves the same purpose as the Blind Cross, but contains certain advantages over it. Because of the Blind Cross it is usually said that right-footers should play the right wing and left-footers should play the left wing. With the Non-Blind Cross, however, the reverse is true. Naturally a player able to kick equally well with both feet can play either side, but in the amateur ranks most players cannot do so and the coach should seriously consider the advantages of this kick over the Blind Cross kick. The Non-Blind Cross is made as follows. A right-footed dribbler moves the ball down the left wing. As she approaches the goal, she starts to cut inwards towards the goal. This move allows the dribbler a full view of the situation in front of the goal. When she spots an unmarked teammate, say on the right side of the goal, she makes a right-footed pass using the Outside-of-the-Foot kick. While doing so, she maintains her vision of the field in front of the goal, except of course during the moment the kick is in process: At the moment of the kick, she must look down at the ball during this time as she would do during the proper execution of any kick. A typical Non-Blind Cross situation is shown in *Illustration 5-5* (see next page).

The Drill

- Each player should practice the Outside-of-the-Foot kick prior to the actual drill.

- Set up the drill as shown in *Figure 5-4* (see page 123).

- The two lines at the Halfway Line are formed such that the right-footed kickers are on the left hand side and left-footed kickers on the right hand side of the field.

Illustration 5-5. A Typical Non-Blind Cross

LEGEND
ball
defenders
attackers
goalkeeper

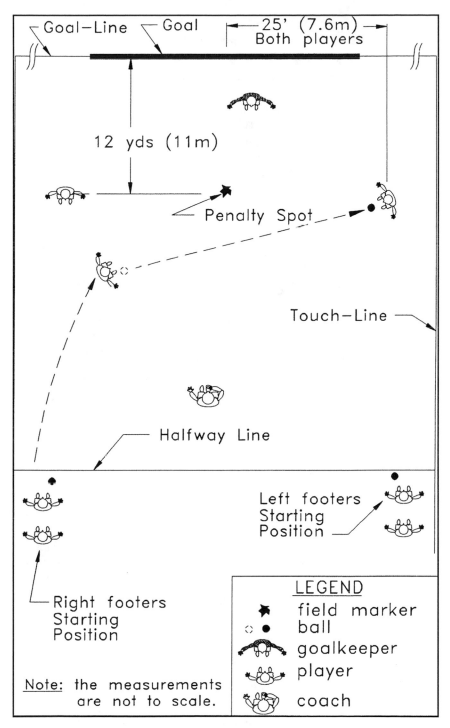

Figure 5-4. The Non-Blind Cross Drill

- The first player from one line is then to dribble the ball down the touch line. As she approaches the level of the field near the penalty spot, she is to cut inwards towards the goal and make the cross to the furthest teammate standing near the front of the goal. A ground pass is ideal. The right-footed cross will go the teammate on the right hand side of the field. The type of kick used in this exercise is the Outside-of-the-Foot kick. *Note:* The field marker locating the penalty spot can be considered as an opponent whose field location would be considered offside for attackers, should they venture past this level before the ball is kicked.

- After the cross is made, the receiving teammate on the opposite side of the field is to join the rear of either line, being replaced by the crossing player. Balance the flow of players to give each player equal tries making crosses, as much as possible.

- The crossing player is to retrieve the ball.

- **The coach should observe the following: The player making the cross should make the cross at some point located just before or at the penalty spot level of the field. She should be looking at the ball during the kick and make the kick such that it does not have a high arc: A ground pass is preferred. Young players should dribble the ball midway between the penalty spot and the touch line on their side.**

- **The coach is to observe that the ball is not kicked near the goalkeeper.**

Drill 5.5
PENALTY KICKS

Penalty Kicks are given for serious defensive infractions occurring to attackers inside of the defenders' penalty area. Penalty kicks are taken from the penalty spot located 12 yards (11 m) from the center of the goal. The only opponent allowed in this play is the goalkeeper, and this individual must remain stationary at the center of the goal until the ball is kicked. Penalty kicks are normally taken by the best goal scorers and are not normally given to the individual who was fouled. The reason is that this individual may have residual emotional feelings from the foul and may thus have less concentration. Penalty kicks are rather difficult to make under pressure and players without recent practice making them probably have a 60-40 chance of success. The success percentage will vary from the suggested 60-40 level, depending upon experience and skill level, but to increase the success level to say 80 percent and above, one needs recent penalty kicking practice.

A good practice for increasing one's accuracy at making the Penalty Kick is by the employment of an aiming technique similar to that of shooting billiards or pool. The technique is as follows: A player places the ball on the penalty spot and picks a targeted point within the goal. This point should be located 2' (0.6 m) towards the center direction from one of the upright goal posts. He then sights over the ball while choosing the spot on the ball that is in direct line with the targeted point in the goal. This is the point on the ball that must be contacted with the foot to accurately propel the ball at the target in the goal. The precise kicking point on the ball enables one to concentrate on focusing only on that point during the kicking procedure. When the ball is kicked at that point, it allows the ball to hit the target providing that no effects from curvature produced by ball spin or wind occur. Without these effects the ball will hit the target if it is kicked straight through the point while being followed through to the target. If kicks are used that cause the ball to curve, the player must compensate for the ball's curved flight trajectory.

Choosing a kick such as the Duck Bill or Push Pass produces no spin (or curvature) if the ball is contacted in a straight line by the foot as well as following through the kick. These two kicks keep the process simple. See *Figure 5-5* for the sighting of the ball. *Note:* For outdoor soccer, the ball should be kept low (aimed for the lower corner of the goal) and for indoor soccer, the ball should be aimed high (aimed for the upper corner of the goal).

The Drill

- Set up the drill according to *Figure 5-5* (see next page).

- The player making the penalty shot is to place the ball on the penalty spot and sight along the ball to the targeted area by moving the ball to align a spot that must be struck with the foot.

- Have the player move back about 5' (1.5 m) after sighting along the ball to the target. *Note 1:* During the alignment, the kicker must disguise the intended kick direction, but should be reminded to

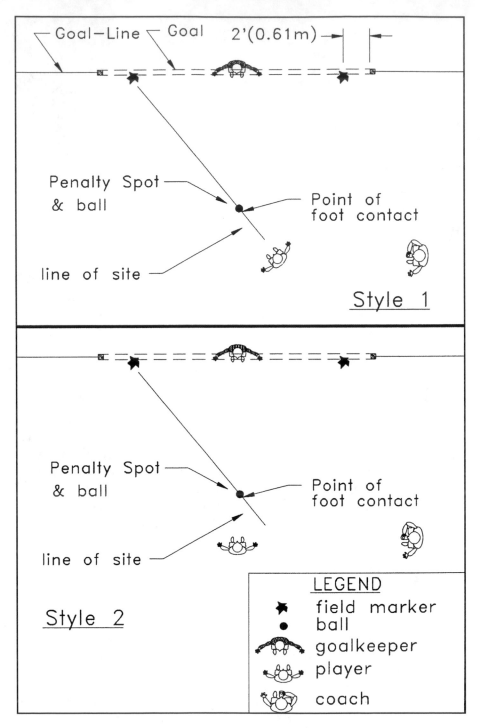

Figure 5-5. The Penalty Kick Drill

always use the same chosen technique and type of kick for all future penalty kicks (i.e., only one method of kicking is all that is necessary for each individual). The infrequency of penalty kicks obviates the necessity of having more than one style. *Note 2:* There are two variations to this style of kicking. The choice is up to the player.

The player may run directly in line with the trajectory of the kick **(Style 1)**. The advantage of running in line with the ball's trajectory gives the kicker the most accuracy, but may indicate to the goalkeeper where the shot is intended. However, a well placed shot is very difficult to defend against.

The player may run directly down the center of the field and kick at the chosen point **(Style 2)**. The advantage of running down the center of the field and kicking to the spot aimed at the corner causes some degree of inaccuracy, but better disguises the kick direction.

- The player is to run up to the ball and kick the chosen spot. The accuracy depends upon keeping one's eyes on the ball, following through the kick and refraining from looking up until the ball is in the back of the net. *Note:* Speed is not necessary if the ball hits its target (within the corner area).

- **The coach is to observe that the player keeps his eyes on the ball and follows through with the kick. The coach should also require that the kick be made with either the Duck Bill or Push Pass kick.**

Drill 5.6
WALLS

Walls are formed to protect the goal against both direct and indirect kicks. They are normally set up and directed by the goalkeeper and he should have at least one training session setting them up in his career. Walls generally employ anywhere from two to five people, depending upon the angle that the ball is kicked from, in reference to the goal. The greater the angle, in reference to a line dividing the field lengthwise, the less the number of wall players that are needed. The wall must be set up at a minimum of 10 yards (9.15 m) in front of the ball, unless the ball is located less than that distance from the goal. In this case, the wall is formed at the goal line. The general idea for the wall is to protect one side of the goal while the

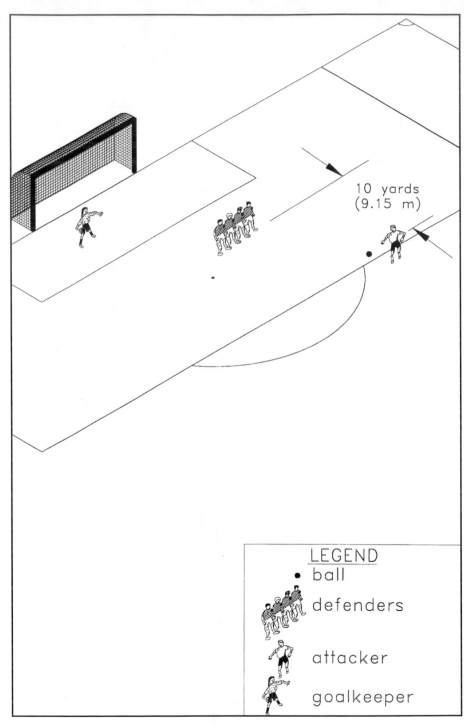

10 yards
(9.15 m)

LEGEND
• ball
defenders
attacker
goalkeeper

Figure 5-6. Walls Drill

goalkeeper covers the other side. The possibility of a ball curving its way around a wall is always present and this must be considered by the goalkeeper.

The Drill

- Set up the drill as shown in *Figure 5-6*. For this wall, four players are needed. Notice that the goalkeeper is standing slightly nearer to the right post (from his perspective). This positioning allows for the possibility of the ball's flight being curved around this end of the wall. The wall players are skewed more towards the goalkeeper's left upright goalpost. *Note:* Wall players generally use two measures of protection: One measure in defense of the goal is to keep their legs sufficiently closed to prevent the ball from passing between the legs. The other measure is for self protection by covering their groin area with their hands before the ball is kicked (this is not illustrated).

- Once the wall has been set up and is satisfactory to the goalkeeper, have three players, who might be chosen in games for the kick, take three kicks each at the goal.

- After these kicks, increase the angle of kick several degrees by moving the ball closer to the left touch line (the goalkeeper's left side). Have the goalkeeper form a wall using one less player in the wall (three players). This concludes the drill. At this point, it is not necessary to make repeated kicks at the goal as the practice time can be better utilized for other drills. This should be sufficient training for making walls.

- **The coach should verify that the goal is protected on the close side by players and on the far side of the wall by the goalkeeper. The goalkeeper should learn to direct this activity.**

Drill 5.7

THE OUTSIDE-OF-THE-FOOT TRAP

The Mechanics

The Outside-of-the-Foot Trap is shown in *Illustration 5-6* (see page 130). This trap is made when a ball is coming at about a 90 degree angle

Illustration 5-6.
The Outside-of-the-Foot Trap

towards the trapper and also at a location where he has to reach out with the leg and foot to contact it.

The trap is made during this drill with the player moving off to either his right or left and finally facing 90 degrees to the ball's incoming direction, as shown in **Stage 3** of *Figure 5-7*. As the ball comes towards the player, he is to go towards it and stop just before reaching out to make the trap. As the player reaches out his foot, he contacts the ball with the top of the toes, or a little farther back on the top of the foot. During the trap the player must keep his eyes on the ball. The ball is to drop dead at the trap site.

After the trap, the player with the ball is to turn around to one of the field markers and dribble the ball back to it. At this point, the player will again turn towards his drill partner and pass the ball back briskly to him at the same angle that he received his pass.

The Drill

- Set up the drill as shown in *Figure 5-7*. The teammates will be 15 to 20' (4.5 m /6 m) apart, depending upon their age and skill level and about 12' (3.7 m) from the adjacent group. For this discussion we have sets of players arranged in five columns. Each pair of players share a ball for the purpose of kicking it back and forth to each other; an odd numbered player will join a pair. The first player is to kick the ball to either of his partner's field markers: The kick direction (the left or right field marker) will depend upon the immediate proximal location of the neighbor's position so as not to interfere with each other. The receiving player in turn will reach out and trap the ball dead at his feet. The drill is performed in the following manner.

  With each pair of players positioned as shown in the figure (using Player #1 and Player #2), *Player #1* kicks the ball to *Player #2's* field marker with sufficient velocity to duplicate a pass in a game. This is **Stage 1**.

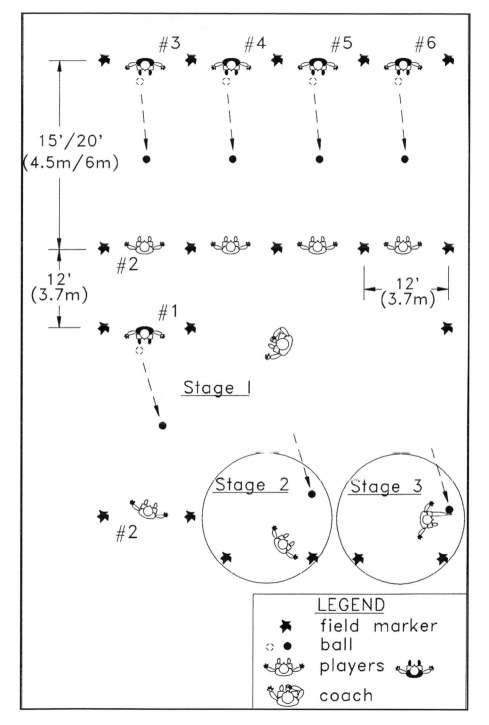

Figure 5-7. The Outside-of-the-Foot Trap Drill

Player #2 goes to the ball as shown in **Stage 2**. Before the trap is made, *Player #2* must stop before reaching for the ball (if possible). This is the beginning of **Stage 3**.

As this player receives the ball, he is to trap the ball with the upper portion of the foot with the top of the toes area, such that it stops in front of the trapping foot. The trapped ball must be controlled with a few extra dribbles before dribbling it back to one of his the field markers. The eyes must be on the ball during the trapping process.

After reaching the field marker, the player then turns around and kicks the ball back to the partner's field marker. *Note:* The ball is to be passed back to the teammate's field marker at a time and location so as not to disturb the adjacent player.

- Run the exercise for about five minutes then rotate the top players (as shown in the figure) of each pair group enabling each player to change partners; i.e., *Player #3* goes to position #4, *Player #4* goes to position #5, *Player #5* goes to position #6 and *Player #6* goes to position #3, etc. Repeat this drill two more times. The total time for the exercise should be approximately 15 minutes.

- **The coach should be observing that the trappers keep their eyes on the ball during trapping, that the ball does not rise just after impact with the foot and that the ball stops just in front of the feet.**

Drill 5.8
THE UNDER-THE-BODY INSTEP KICK

The Mechanics

The Under-the-Body Instep Kick shown in *Illustration 5-7* is a variation of the Angled Instep Kick. The difference for the usage of the two kicks is as follows: The Instep Kick or the Angled Instep Kick are usually executed by running up to the ball prior to making the kick, as with goal kicks, corner kicks, etc. Younger players also use the Instep or Angled Instep Kicks to score goals, especially when there is little or no resistance from opponents. However, this method of kicking the ball is not very useful when an able opponent is near—one that is kicked from under the body is preferred.

As shown in this left-footed illustration, this kick requires that the nonkicking right foot be placed alongside of the ball with the toes of this foot located at the front of it. Also the nonkicking foot is placed 6 to 12 inches (15 to 30 cm) to the side of the ball. This is not a natural action and a conscious effort must be made to place the nonkicking foot towards the front of the ball. If it is desired to place the ball in the air, then the toe of the nonkicking foot is not placed as far forward.

To produce a good kick, the head must be kept down with the eyes fixed on the ball during the entire kicking process. It is necessary to follow through the kick to obtain both power and accuracy. The kicking foot should follow a straight line during the kick. The ball must not be kicked in an arched fashion or accuracy will generally be sacrificed. When this kick is utilized, the ball is not kicked in its center. It is kicked slightly off center and this motion to the ball causes it to spin. As a result of the spin, the

Illustration 5-7.
The Under-the-Body
Instep Kick

ball curves in that same direction. With a left-footed kick, the ball will curve to the right while a right-footed kick will cause the ball to curve to the left. To attain accuracy the player must compensate for the spin.

The Drills

The Under-the-Body Instep Kick drill is performed in two versions.

Version 1 (Static Situation)

- Set up the drill as shown in *Figure 2-1* (see page 19).

- The goals are placed at B 20' (6 m) from the field markers containing the players. Note that Location C is not used for this stage of the drill.

- For this stage, the player is to kick a stationary ball through the goal following the kicking procedure outlined above.

    As normal, the player is not to immediately look up after the ball is kicked.

The player may only look up after the ball passes the goal.

Each player gets three kicks and three rotational turns.

After each player gets her turn, she is to retrieve the balls.

- **The coach should be checking that the placement of the nonkicking foot is located at the front of the ball and that the kickers are keeping eyes on the ball during the entire kick.**

Version 2 (Dynamic Situation)

- This drill allows players to make kicks at the goal while dribbling the ball. It is more practical and should only be substituted for Version 1 when the players are performing the static shooting on goal satisfactorily and have been exposed to dribbling drills.

- Place a set of 4 field markers at C 10' (3 m) behind the field markers A.

- All players are now to stand behind the field markers at C.

- Each player is to dribble the ball to the field markers at B and take a shot at the goal. As above, the players are not to look up until the shot has reached at the goal.

- **The coach should be watching to determine that the ball is kept near the feet prior to the kick.**

- **The coach should also be looking to determine that the kickers are keeping their eyes on the ball during the entire kick and that the nonkicking foot is located at the front of the ball.**

Drill 5.9

HEAD TRAPPING

The Mechanics

Whenever the circumstances permit one to do so, head trapping a soccer ball should be the preferable choice between trapping the ball or heading the ball up field. The trap places your team on the offense, while heading frequently turns over the ball to the opponents.

There are two versions of this trap. The easiest to employ is somewhat in between the headed ball and the trap. This version, the slowing down of the ball and at the same time executing a short pass to a nearby teammate's feet, allows the teammate to easily get control of the ball. This method (deflecting the ball to a teammate) generally does not require practice when the players are conditioned to playing ball control soccer. The second method, however, is slightly more difficult to perform and it is the one that is the focus of this drill.

Illustration 5-8.
Head Trapping

Head trapping the ball is performed by absorbing the ball's impact with the head, neck and back. See *Illustration 5-8*. In the illustration, Number 1 indicates the arrival of the ball. The ball is contacted at the lower center of the forehead with the eyes open and on the ball at all times in a similar fashion as with the headed ball, except the back does not propel the ball. With the head, neck and back recoiling with the ball's impact, the ball is then slowed down and will rise slightly as indicated by Number 2. It then drops (Number 3) and is placed under control with the body. As in heading, keeping one's eyes open during the time of contact is difficult for novice soccer players; therefore, the ball should be thrown to these players at a moderate speed. As players progress with this skill, they can receive faster balls.

The drill is performed by lobbing the ball to the player's head. The player is to contact the ball with the head while slowing down its motion by the backward thrusting of the head, neck and back.

Note: This trap requires more time to settle the ball than with foot traps, due to the large dropping distance of the ball from the head to the ground. Thus it is a difficult trap to make near an opponent as the trapper must wait for the ball to drop before making the next move. Therefore, it is imperative for the trapper to turn his back to the opponent as soon as he has control of the ball (as the ball is dropping).

The thrower is to apply pressure on the trapper after making the throw.

The Drill

- Arrange the players as shown in *Figure 5-8* (see next page). The distance can vary depending upon the players' ages and abilities.

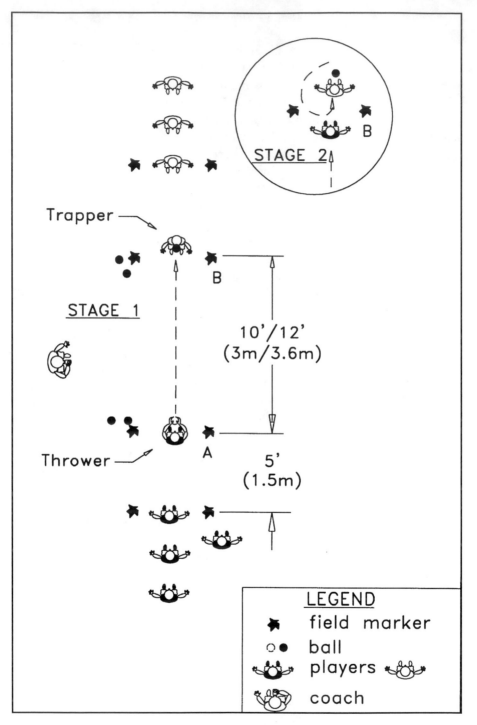

Figure 5-8. The Head Trapping Drill

- The player located at A is to throw the ball to the player located at B. The throw is made underhanded by starting at the knee level and throwing with both hands. This is shown in **Stage 1**.

- The receiving player is to head trap the ball by cushioning it with the recoil described above (the ball should not rise too high).

- As the trapping begins, the thrower (the opponent) is to apply pressure to the trapper by running to the trapping player to attempt to remove the ball from him.

- The trapper must shield the ball by turning 180 degrees as the ball comes under control, as shown in **Stage 2**. While doing so he then dribbles it away from the opponent.

- Each player is to trap the ball three times, if done correctly. If the head trapping is not done correctly or the throws are imprecise, repeat the throws until each player makes three correct traps. After three good traps the trapping player is to return to the end of the opposite line.

- The drill continues with the thrower moving back to the front of his original line (in this case the line located at A). This player now waits for the throw from the player located at B.

- The drill should last for 15 minutes.

- **The coach is to observe that the player gets to control the ball and shields it.**

- **It is also important that the coach observe that the player's eyes remain open during the trap.**

5b. Mid-Advanced Drills— Intermediate Defensive

Drill 5.10
PERSON TO PERSON DEFENSE IN THE DEFENSIVE AREA

The Mechanics

Strict defensive habits are of paramount importance. The purpose of this drill is to instruct wing defenders and the goalkeeper on a proper defensive formation. The two techniques outlined in this drill require that wing defenders be in position at all times (not getting caught out of position by venturing too far up field) and always remain goal-side of their attacking wing opponents in their territory. Along with this, it is stressed that defense of the goal is probably the single most important measure needed for winning soccer games.

Coaches that only half believe in proper defensive measures can give lip service to players by only espousing that defense is important. In reality however, they may place all or most of the emphasis on attack strategy. This approach to soccer is short sighted. Very often games are lost by just one goal and these goals are frequently scored via the wings. This location on the field is generally overlooked due to an emphasis on security directly in front of the goal at the time that it is besieged. Confusion in the center due to opponent penetration or a shot at the goal (missed or scored) often follows from unstructured wing defense. This defensive disarray on the wings often causes other defensive players to scramble about in front of the goal in haphazard panic. This confusion can be frequently prevented when the attacking wing players each properly guard their attacking wingers, thus hampering organized opponent attacks.

It should be remembered that defensive players are defensive players. Too often these players (and the coach) do not completely understand their role on the field and the defensive players play too far up field to try to assist in the scoring activities. This type of strategy usually causes defending players to be out of formation when a counterattack on their goal begins. These players must then run at full speed in pursuit of their attackers as these and other attacking players penetrate their defense. A good defense, however, starts with the wing defenders effectively neutralizing these attacking wingers by not being caught out of position by being too far up field. When this occurs the goalkeeper can concentrate on the middle of the field near the goal, confident that the defensive wingers are correctly doing their job by neutralizing their attacking wingers. Furthermore, as the goalkeeper observes unmarked attacking players he would then call back other players to cover them.

In summary, this drill requires that the wing defenders learn to not wander too far up field to efficiently neutralize the attacking wingers. When they are out of position it is the responsibility of the goalkeeper to effectively remind his defense of their job. This drill also gives the goalkeeper leadership practice at full defensive coverage: He will be practicing with defensive players as he learns to also call in other players on the scene to cover any unguarded attacking players.

The Drill

- Set up the drill as shown in *Figure 5-9* (see next page).

- The drill starts with three attacking players moving up field, from Locations A1, A2 and A3 from the Halfway Line. This is **Stage 1**. They are heading up field with the center player dribbling the ball towards the goal mouth. The attacking wing players must remain slightly behind the attacker with the ball. If they do not, the drill must be restarted. *Note:* This figure is not to scale.

- Immediately after the drill begins, two defenders from Location D3 run to Locations D1 and D2 to cover the wing players while leaving the dribbler unmarked. When these defenders reach their attacking players, they are to get goal side of their opponent and remain that way for the duration of the drill. When they back up to within 10' (3 m) of the goal they are to stop and hold their ground.

- With the attacking wingers now neutralized, the goalkeeper is to call to the next player at the head of the line at Location D3 to pick up the player with the ball. This is **Stage 2**. The situation is now as

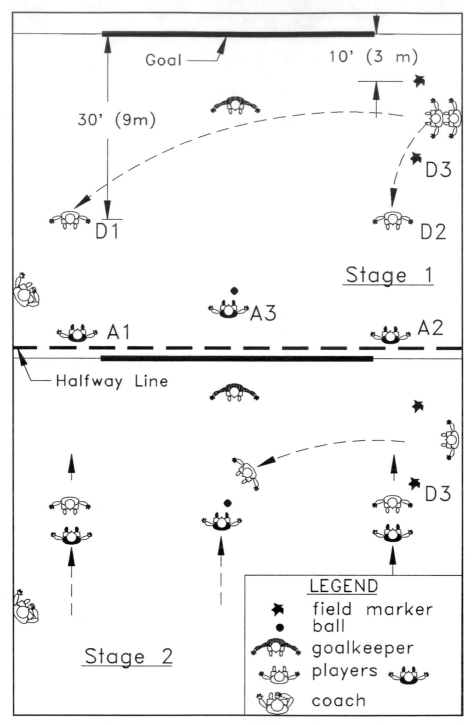

Figure 5-9. Person to Person Defense Drill

follows: The goalkeeper is to observe the conditions in his defensive area. If all attacking players are not neutralized, he is to send out corrective instructions to any of the defenders if they falter in their duties. The attackers, on the other hand, may do whatever is necessary to endeavor to score a goal.

- The attack is over when the play is either destroyed or a goal is scored. Repeat the drill with a new set of attackers and defenders and continue the attack/defense process for the duration of the drill.

- The duration of this drill is 15 minutes.

- **The coach is to observe that the wing defenders neutralize their opponents by remaining constantly goal side of these opponents and that the goalkeeper takes command of the defense.**

6a. Advanced Field Drills — Offensive

Drill 6.1

ONCE-ON KICK

The Mechanics

A Once-On Kick is a term used to describe a kick at the goal where the player is not in possession of the ball, but is near enough to move to the ball and kick it at the goal. It is the subject of this drill and utilizes a rolling ground pass across the goal mouth. The ground pass can be either thrown, or kicked with a Push-Pass by the coach after the player rushes at the goal. With the player rushing at the goal, the coach propels the ball on the ground in front of the attacking player as he continues to rush at the ball to once-on kick it past the goalkeeper. The type of kick used by the attacking player in this drill is the Push-Pass kick.

It is a requirement of this drill to utilize the Push-Pass kick at close range to the goal: Using other types of once on kicks at a rolling ball can be very inaccurate, especially if the ball takes an unexpected hop. A very common and poor practice is to have the players make the kick from a long distance out in front of the goal: This practice teaches players how not to score goals. The idea behind this drill is to get each player's scoring confidence up by allowing them to have a high success rate of scoring.

The success rate for goal scoring technique in games will depend upon each player developing confidence gained by concentration and having many experiences of kicking the ball past the goalkeeper.

Note: The goalkeeper will not like this drill.

The Drill

- Set up the drill as shown in *Figure 6-1.*

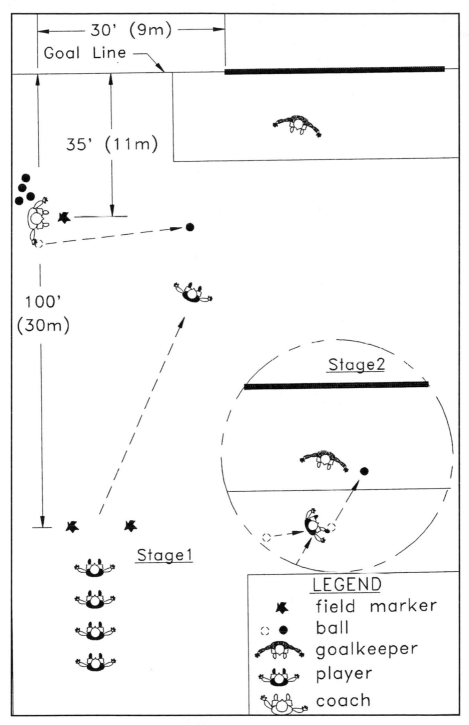

30' (9m)

Goal Line

35' (11m)

100'
(30m)

Stage2

Stage1

LEGEND

★ field marker

○ ● ball

goalkeeper

player

coach

Figure 6-1. The Once-On Kick Drill

- The first player at the head of the line is to rush towards the goal as shown in **Stage 1**.

- The coach is then to roll or push pass the ball at a medium speed in front of the goal mouth.

- The player heads for the ball to meet it and make a once-on Push Pass kick past the goalkeeper, and into the goal as shown in **Stage 2**.

- Each player is to get two chances at scoring via the once-on kick. After the second kick at the goal, the player is to retrieve the balls and return to the end of the line.

- The drill should take place for 15 minutes.

- **The coach should determine that the players are properly making a correct Push-Pass kick by keeping their eyes on the ball and following though the kick.**

Drill 6.2
THE TOE-POKE KICK

The Mechanics

It is frequently stated that soccer players should not use their toe to kick the ball. This is generally true, but not always. One exception to this rule is with the Toe-Poke kick shown in *Illustration 6-1*. This kick is useful under certain conditions to score goals. One such condition is as follows: Say a player is alone in front of the goal and has control of the ball. As she nears the goalkeeper, the goalkeeper runs out to attempt to foil a potential

Illustration 6-1. The Toe-Poke Kick

shot at the goal. As the goalkeeper nears the ball, the player pokes the ball with her toe (rather slowly and on the ground) to one of the corners of the goal. If the ball is kept low, speed is not important provided the Toe-Poke

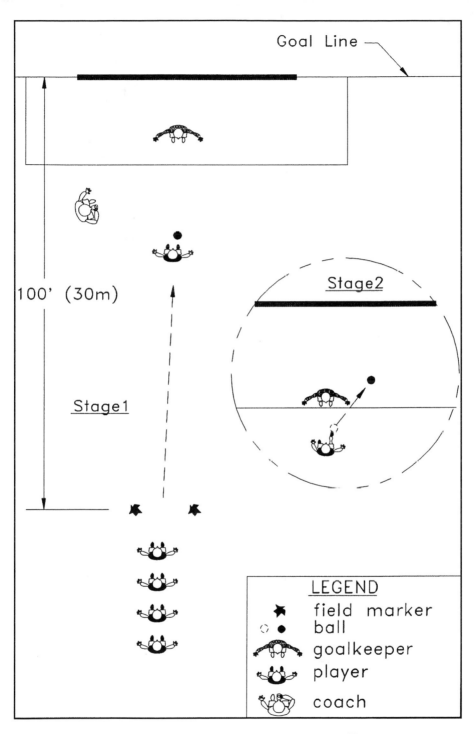

Goal Line

100' (30m)

Stage2

Stage1

LEGEND

★ field marker
○ ● ball
goalkeeper
player
coach

Figure 6-2. The Toe-Poke Kick Drill

kick is executed while the goalkeeper is at a distance of about 2 to 4' (0.6 to 1.2 m) from the ball and that there is a clear passage to one of the corners of the goal. The drill is performed by the dribbling player coming into the goal area on a one-to-one encounter with the goalkeeper. As the dribbling player approaches the goal, the Toe-Poke kick is made at the right moment.

The Drill

- Set up the drill as shown in *Figure 6-2* (see previous page).

- The player at the head of the line is to dribble the ball up the center of the field towards the goal and the goalkeeper. This is **Stage 1**.

- As the dribbler nears the goalkeeper, he (the goalkeeper) is to come off of his line (the 5' [1.5 m] point in the front of the goal) to attempt to remove the ball from the dribbler as shown in **Stage 2**.

- As the dribbler nears the goal, she is to poke the ball past the goalkeeper into either corner of the goal. The dribbler must keep her eyes on the ball during the kick and follow through with the kick.

- At the completion of the shot, the player is to retrieve the ball and join the end of the line.

- Each player is to get three separate tries at scoring.

- **The coach is to observe that the Toe-Poke kick is performed at the correct distance (as mentioned above) and that the kicker keeps her eyes on the ball and follows through with the kick.**

Drill 6.3

DRIBBLING FAKE FOR PASSING AN OPPONENT

The Mechanics

The Dribbling Fake for Passing an Opponent is used to pass a single opponent while dribbling. The drill and this tactic require that the ball be

dribbled close to the body and made in the following manner. If a dribbling player is generally in open space on the field and being challenged
by an opponent, the dribbler can decide to fake to one side of the opponent and pass her on his other side with a self-pass, providing that there is
sufficient space around and behind the opponent to recover the ball after
the fake and self-pass.

When the dribbler approaches the opponent or the opponent is backing up with the dribbler, the dribbler shifts into a lower gear by slowing
down and using only one foot for pushing the ball. The scenario prior to
the fake is depicted in *Illustration 2-9* (see page 48) by a player dribbling
the ball with one foot while being impeded by a defending opponent. The
dribbler, having chosen to fake at a particular side of the opponent, dribbles with the foot on that same side. As he dribbles the ball with only this
foot, he pushes the ball with every step. This is **Stage 1** as shown in *Figure 6-3* (see page 148). If he chooses to pass on the right side, the body
feint will go to his left side but the ball will go to his right side. The situation is reversed for the left sided passing maneuver.

As an example, after deciding which side to pass, the dribbler will
change-up the pace to dribble the ball with one foot on that same side, contacting the ball only with the top of the toes. At the moment the dribbler
decides to make his fake (for this example he chooses to go to his right
side), his weight will be shifted to his left foot. He then simultaneously
thrusts his body to the left side in a feinting move by pivoting off of the
right foot to give the appearance that he is moving to his left side (the
opponent's right side). This is **Stage 2**. *Note 1*: If the opponent improperly
defends by accepting the fake as a genuine move to her right (the dribbler's left), her reflex action will shift her own balance to her right (the
dribbler's left). This out-of-balance move is just what the dribbler is waiting for; however, if she defends properly and does not buy the fake, the
fake must be aborted.

If the feinting move is successful, the next move is to flick the ball to
the dribbler's right side via the top of the right foot at a 45 degree angle
to the direction of the run. This is **Stage 3**. This self-pass is made with the
foot in the same manner as the dribble, i.e., with the top of the toes. With
the opponent accepting the fake, the dribbler then leaps off of the left foot
(his balance is maintained), he then goes to his right and receives his self-
pass. This is **Stage 4**. *Note 2*: The ball's speed off the self-pass must be
of the proper speed: If it is too slow, the defender can recover, foiling the
fake. If it is too fast the dribbler will have to chase the ball too far, ren-
dering the move to pass the opponent useless. The angle of the self-pass

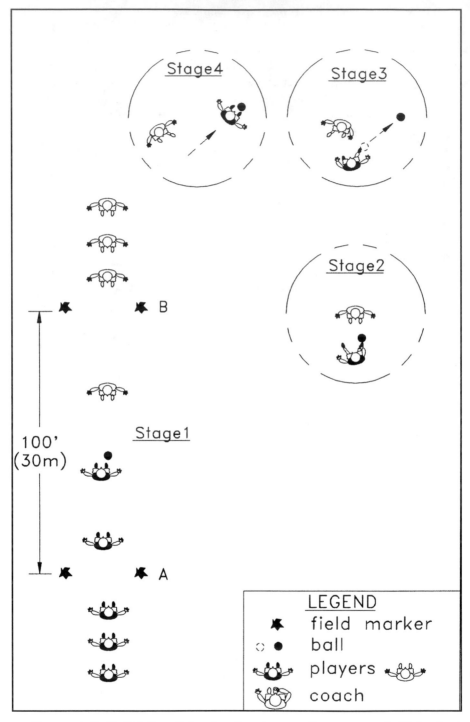

Figure 6-3. Dribbling Fake for Passing an Opponent Drill (v. 1)

must be approximately 45 degrees. The above fake is to be made in Version 1 below.

In Version 2, a shot at the goal is added to the fake: The fake will be made as above, but instead of recovering the ball for dribbling, a shot at the goal will take place at the first re-contact of the ball.

Version 1 (Passing an Opponent)

- Set up the drill as shown in *Figure 6-3*.

- Make two identical columns of players containing one-quarter of the team on either end of each column (only one column is shown in the figure). The two groups will allow players to get more time on the ball.

- The first player of each line at Location A begins by dribbling the ball toward the defending opponent coming off of the line at Location B as shown in **Stage 1**.

- As the player approaches the opponent, he is to slow down and begin to dribble with one foot—the right foot is used when planning to go to the right and the left foot is used when planning to go to the left.

- The dribbler then approaches near the opponent (who, in this drill, does not attempt to take the ball from novices learning to make the fake). He continues to dribble, shifts the dribbling to only one foot and makes the fake as shown in **Stage 2**. He then flicks the ball in the opposite direction for the self-pass as in **Stage 3**.

- The dribbler then chases the ball as shown in **Stage 4**, retrieves it and dribbles it towards the direction of the goal (the goal is not shown in the figure). The drill is now complete.

- The player then recovers the ball and gets two more chances before moving to the end of the opposite line from which he emerged. The defender also joins the opposite line.

- If this drill is repeated with experienced players, slightly increase the defensive pressure.

- **The coach is to observe the following. The dribbling player is to slow down and dribble the ball with the same foot as the side of the self-pass. The player is to reduce his speed sufficiently to enable him to execute a plausible and flawless fake. The player is also to keep his eyes on the ball during the flick (self-pass).**

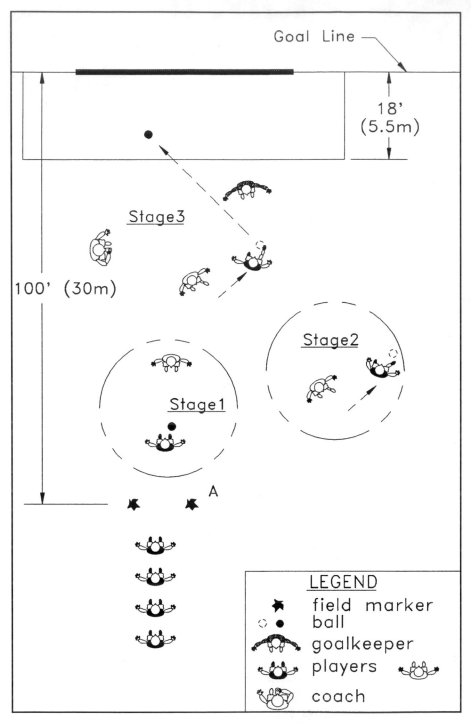

Goal Line

18'
(5.5m)

Stage3

100' (30m)

Stage2

Stage1

A

LEGEND
★ field marker
◌ ● ball
goalkeeper
players
coach

Figure 6-3. Dribbling Fake for Passing an Opponent Drill (v. 2)

Version 2 (Passing an Opponent and a Shot at the Goal)

This drill is similar to Version 1 except that after the fake, the dribbler takes a first time kick at the ball with the purpose of beating the goalkeeper.

- This drill uses one defensive player, a goalkeeper, one column of players and a goal. Set up the drill as shown *Figure 6-4.*

- The dribbling player leaves location A and approaches the defender located initially midway between the goal and location A. This is **Stage 1**.

- The defender in this drill approaches the dribbler and then backs up with the attacker. When the situation is just right for the dribbler, approximately 6' (1.8 m) before the 18' (5.5 m) line, she fakes to one side and self-passes to the other side. This is **Stage 2**. *Note:* The defender's pressure is minimal as the purpose of this drill is to teach the fake with a shot at the goal.

- The self-pass must be such that the dribbler is able to contact the ball and take a shot at the goal on first contact with the ball. A second contact with the ball is not permitted. This is shown in **Stage 3**.

- Each attacking player is to get two chances before returning to the rear of the same line.

- After three or four minutes of defending, rotate the defending players with players that will normally be defenders.

- If another goalkeeper is available, rotate this player also.

- If this drill is repeated with experienced players, slightly increase the defensive pressure.

- **The coach is to observe that the fake is done correctly as in the above drill and that the ball is contacted the first time for the shot on goal.**

Drill 6.4.
TEAM THROW-IN

The Mechanics

This drill focuses mainly on offensive play after the throw, but also describes defensive play.

Offensive Play

In order to improve the team's chances of remaining in possession of the ball after it is thrown out onto the near field, throw-ins require a pre-arranged systematic effort to better the team's chances of retaining ball possession. This drill demonstrates and instructs the team on the necessity of the teamwork effort needed for throw-ins. It also instructs players on how to recognize bad throw-in plays. This drill, an extension of Drill 2.9 (see page 45), takes over where that drill leaves off, thus adding continuity to the complete throw-in play. It utilizes seven players: the thrower, three offensive teammates and three defensive opponents.

The throw-in play goes as follows: The thrower throws the ball to any teammate, preferably to the receiver's feet. As an alternate throw, the ball may be thrown to the receiver's head with the intention of getting the ball back to the thrower immediately. During the time of the throw, realistic opposition will be present as each attacker (with the exception of the thrower) will have an opponent at his back.

The first receiver of the throw shields the ball (this comes naturally if an opponent is behind his back), settles it, or the receiver passes it back to the thrower: The receiver may use this alternate move and immediately pass the ball back to the thrower; normally, however, the receiver would settle the ball, dribble it or pass it to any open teammate. If the first receiver does not settle it, the thrower must settle it. *Note 1:* This is one of the few occasions in ball control soccer where the receiver does not settle the ball.

With either the first receiver or the thrower settling the ball, this person is then to look for an open player to pass to (the ball may be passed in any direction). This should easily occur since there is a one-player advantage over the defensive team. *Note 2:* It is important to understand that during this drill, or in games, the play is not considered over until one player clearly has the ball under control. This is necessary to comprehend, otherwise the concept of retaining possession of the ball is not grasped.

Defensive Play

Defensive Play on throw-ins require that *all* opponents be marked by any of your team's players. They are to remain behind the player during the throw-in process until the ball is settled by, or passed from, the first receiving player. After this point in time, the defenders may choose to move about anywhere that is considered necessary. *Note:* During your competitive games, this defensive coverage will increase your offensive play as you will obtain ball possession more often.

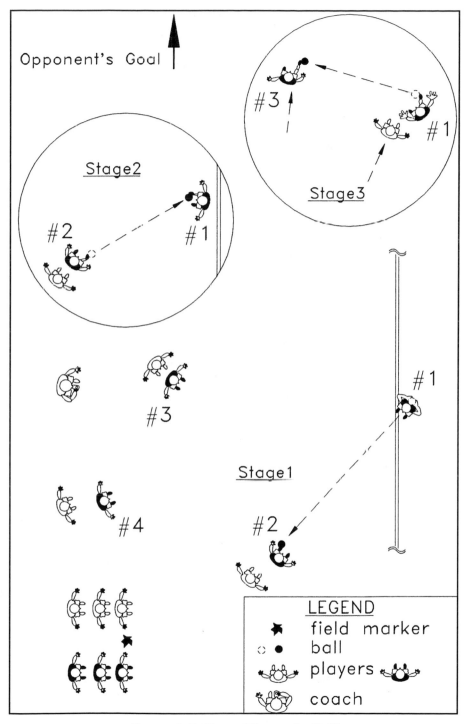

Figure 6-5. Team Throw-In Drill

The Drill

- Set up the drill as shown in *Figure 6-5* (see previous page). Prior to the throw-in, the three defensive players are to each cover an offensive player.

- The thrower (**Player #1**) then throws the ball to any teammate such as **Player #2**. This player is to chose whether or not to pass the ball back to the unmarked thrower (**Player #1**) as described above or to either **Player #3** or **Player #4**. The next receiving teammate is to endeavor to settle the ball while shielding it from the opponent.

- If the ball has been returned to the thrower, he is then to settle it. In the meantime, the defenders may now move about anywhere to intercept the ball.

- With the four to three advantage over the defensive players, the offense will always have an open player and should have no difficulty in maintaining ball possession. The ball is to be passed about by each player, but only after each player has settled the ball first. *Note:* Single or double touch playing is only acceptable with the original receiver.

- The play is over when one offender gets up field with the ball or the defenders intercept the ball.

- Repeat the drill by rotating all defensive players and all offensive players such that they all get to make a throw-in.

- After each offensive and defensive player plays the position of Player #4, they are to join the opposing team's line, i.e., the offender joins the rear of the defensive line and vice versa.

- **The coach is to observe both the offense and defense to see that they follow the principles outlined above. It is important to understand that during this drill, or in a game situation, the throw-in is only successful if your team ends up with the ball by mounting an offensive: To determine this, one needs to learn to recognize which team actually ends up with the ball after several plays on the ball.**

Drill 6.5
Three Person Attack on Goal/Wing Follow-Up

The Mechanics

This drill is designed to make forward players cognizant of a need to follow up the attack when there is an attack or a shot at the goal. A common practice with forward players is to slacken off their attack when one of their teammates assaults the goal. Fairly often this assault causes the ball to come out free in front of the goal, especially to the right or left side of it. During competitive games, it can frequently be heard "there was no one there," meaning that the ball became dangerously loose in front of the goal. Players need practice and awareness for the attack continuation at the goal when they do not have the ball.

The drill is as follows: Three players mount an attack on the goal without the ball. As the players arrive, the coach sends the ball across the goal mouth. All three attackers are to continue to run at the goal simulating that the ball has been deflected out by the goalkeeper or hit the goalpost. The first two players do not contact the ball and let it pass them. The third attacker, the right winger, is to take a once-on Push-Pass kick at the goal or, if he is not able to do so, trap the ball and either take a shot on goal or pass it to a teammate for one of them to take the shot at the goal. After the attack, all three players rotate positions.

The Drill

- Set up the drill according to *Figure 6-6* (see next page).

- The first three players in line (***Players #1, #2*** and ***#3***) are to start the attack as shown in the figure.

- When the players come into proximity of the goal, the coach is to pass the ball (nearly parallel to the goal) in front of all players as shown in **Stage 1**.

- *Players #1* and *#2* are to avoid the ball (they may have to jump over it) as shown in **Stages 1 and 2**.

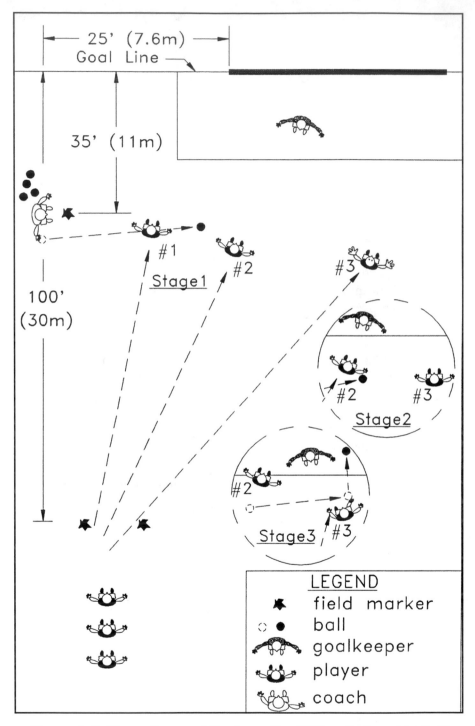

Figure 6-6. Three Person Attack on Goal/Wing Follow-Up Drill

- *Player #3* gets to make the kick as shown in **Stage 3**.

    This player is then to either take a once-on kick (with a Push-Pass), trap the ball (and take the shot), or pass to a teammate.

    The play is over with a scored goal or the ball goes out of play.

- At the end of each drill, rotate all three players. Repeat this drill two more times, then replace all three players with the next three players on line. Do this until all team players have had a turn playing all three positions.

- If the drill is repeated the same day or another day, change over to the right wing side of the field, etc.

- **The coach is to observe that all players continue to press forward during the attack.**

Drill 6.6

TWO PERSON ATTACK ON GOAL

This drill is a sort of a breakaway condition except there is a single defender left at the goal. During this drill, the dribbler is assisted by a teammate to form a two to one advantage over the defender. With or without a defender in front of the goal, when an attacking player is dribbling towards the goal he should always consider passing the ball to another player, if one exists nearby. Too often, a player foolishly tries to score on his own and fails. The defense consists of a defender and the goalkeeper.

The attackers, with a two to one advantage over the defender, are taught to be cognizant of the advantage they have over the single player attack; and thus promote assisting players to co-attack the goal when they might prefer to rest. As stated above, if the attacker were to be alone, defensive pressure could easily cause him to make what could be a bad attempt at a goal shot. The assisting teammate, keeping up with the dribbler but slightly behind him, must signal the dribbler by calling to the attacker that he has help if needed, i.e., in a game breakaway condition, the dribbler with an opponent at his heels may not be aware of an assisting teammate, without his verbal signal. As the dribbler reaches the field marker in front of the goal he is to send a pass in front of the goal to his assistant. In this drill, the unmarked attacking partner has a better chance at scoring a goal.

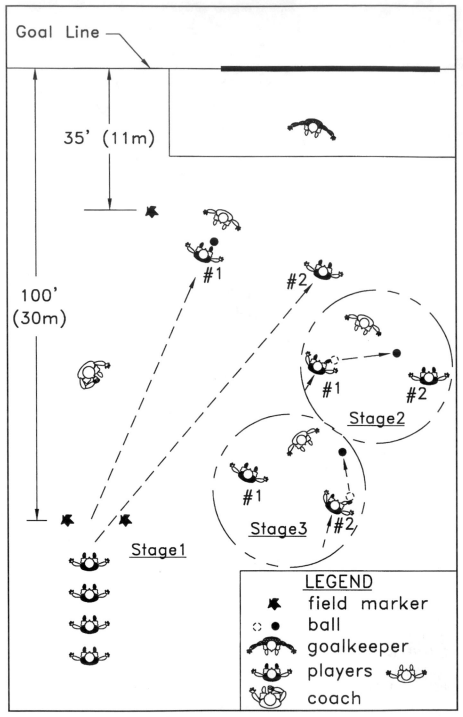

Goal Line

35' (11m)

100'
(30m)

#1

#2

#1

#2

Stage2

#1

Stage3

#2

Stage1

LEGEND
field marker
ball
goalkeeper
players
coach

Figure 6-7. Two Person Attack on Goal

The Drill

- Set up the drill as shown in *Figure 6-7*. The first player in line (**Player #1**) is the attacker with the ball. The second player (**Player #2**) is his assistant. The third player (the defender) is one of your defending players. He is located near the field marker near the goal. At the start of the drill both attackers, the dribbler and his assistant, begin from the line and race down the field towards the goal. This is **Stage 1**.

- When **Player #1** reaches the defender, he is to pass the ball in front of **Player #2** at about an 80 degree angle from the direction of the run, as shown in **Stage 2**.

- **Player #2** then cither makes a Push-Pass kick at the goal or, if it becomes necessary, traps the ball and takes a shot at the goal, as shown in **Stage 3**.

- Repeat this drill by replacing the assistant (**Player #2**). The assistant (the player taking the shot on goal) is then to join the rear of the line.

- The drill is complete after all forward and midfielder players have played in the position of **Player #1** and **#2** three times. If the overall drill is repeated, run the drill from the other side of the field with the assisting attacker (**Player #2**) now on the left side.

- Periodically replace your defending players in the defensive position.

- **The coach is to observe that the dribbler endeavors to make the pass to a point in front of the assistant, where he may easily make a once-on kick without losing his stride. The coach must also determine that the defender does not attack the ball when defending against** ***Player #1.***

Drill 6.7

Halfback and Wing Overlap with Shot

This drill instructs players on the overlap technique. It uses three attackers, one defender and a goalkeeper. Reference *Figure 6-8* (see next page). The attackers consist of a forward left winger, a halfback left winger and

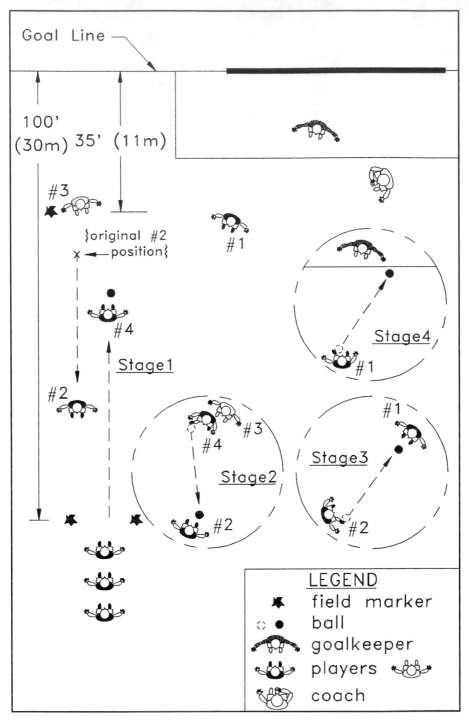

Goal Line

100'
(30m) 35' (11m)

#3

{original #2
position}

#4

Stage1

#1

Stage4

#2

#3

#4

Stage2

Stage3

#1

#2

#2

LEGEND
★ field marker
○ ● ball
goalkeeper
players
coach

Figure 6-8. Halfback and Wing Overlap Drill

a center forward along with a defender that stays near the left wing area. While the employment of only one defender may be unrealistic, it would be too restrictive to teach the overlap technique with too much resistance. The play is as follows: Prior to the start of the drill, two players move off the line and move up to the positions of *center forward* = *Player #1* and the *left forward wing* = *Player #2*, at the X. The third player in line then moves out to become the *defender* = *Player #3*, located at the right forward wing. This is the beginning of **Stage 1**.

At the start of the drill, the fourth player, the *left halfback* = *Player #4* in line then dribbles the ball up to the left wing position to the field marker (near defender #3), moving through his mid-field position into the left wing area to become the temporary left forward winger. He then is met by the defender (*Player #3*). In the meantime, the forward left winger (*Player #2*) moves back down field to cover the vacant left halfback position by overlapping. Since the temporary left winger (*Player #4*) has met defensive resistance and is not able to make an effective cross, he passes the ball back to the temporary left halfback (*Player #2*), shown in **Stage 2**. This player, in turn, receives the ball and passes it to the center forward (*Player #1*), as shown in **Stage 3**. The center forward receives the ball and takes a shot at the goal, as shown in **Stage 4**. *Note:* The center forward player must be careful as not to put himself in an offside position.

The Drill

- Set up the drill as shown in *Figure 6-8*. *Player #1* moves from the line to stand in front of the goal, but down field from the defender as to not be offside. *Player #2* moves to the X location, just in front of the field marker. The defender (*Player #3*) is to stand near the field marker.

- At the start of the drill, **Stage 1**, the left halfback winger (*Player #4*) dribbles the ball up the wing.

- As he dribbles up the wing, the left forward winger (*Player #2*) runs back to overlap into the halfback position.

- When *Player #4* arrives at the forward wing, he is met by the defender who holds his ground to disallow a pass or cross to be made to the front of the goal.

- *Player #4* then passes the ball back to the temporary left halfback (*Player #2*), as shown in **Stage 2**.

- *Player #2* goes to the ball, traps it and passes it to the center forward (*Player #1*), as shown in **Stage 3**.

- *Player #1* in turn goes to the ball, traps it, then takes a shot at the goal, as shown in **Stage 4**.

- After the completion of the play, *Player #1* becomes *Player #2, Player #2* becomes *Player #3, Player #3* becomes *Player #1*. The original *Player #1* joins the rear of the line. The drill continues with a new *Player #4*. Complete the drill when all players get a turn playing each position. If the drill is repeated, perform the drill at the right wing side of the field.

- Periodically replace your defending players in the defensive position.

- **The coach is to observe that the overlapping sequence of events takes place as described above.**

Drill 6.8

KICKOFF WITH OVERLAPPING WING POSITIONS

The kickoff should have a set play. Since this is the only time during a game that all positions of all players are known, it makes good sense to do so. This drill demonstrates an ideal kickoff play ending with a cross pass—a chance at scoring directly from the kickoff. Generally, however, during the kickoff portion of an actual game situation, there is often confusion as to which direction the ball should go. Players should have a structured kickoff play because often amateurs, especially young players who receive the kicked-off ball, immediately press forward towards the goal and dribble up the center of the field. Anomalously, they may even score at this time. If this occurs, onlookers may think that this was a spectacular move on the part of the scoring player and encourage such self-centered playing. This is not a good move against experienced defenses.

The general rule on a kickoff, however, is that when players press forward immediately, they usually turn over the ball to a formidable opponent, because at this time the opponents are in their best defensive position. The best kickoff attack strategy comes from teamwork, control and the initial movement of the ball towards one's own defending goal. Next it should be sent out to one of the wings.

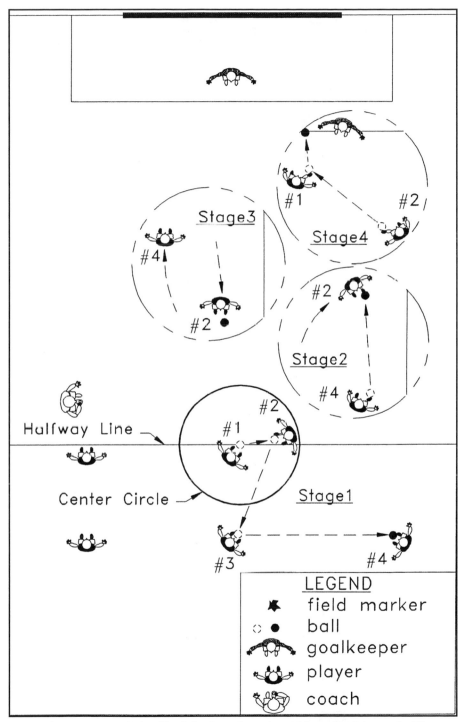

Figure 6-9. Kickoff with Overlapping Wing Positions Drill

The recommended play with reference to *Figure 6-9* (see previous page) is as follows: Shortly after the kickoff from the center forward (***Player #1***), the ball moves forward to the forward right wing (***Player #2***): The ball has been legally kicked off after it moves forward by the distance of its own circumference. This is **Stage 1**. The receiving right winger (***Player #2***), takes the ball but does not press forward. He immediately passes it back to the center halfback (***Player #3***) and with good reason: Halfbacks have more time and space than the forwards to make the next move, and the center halfback can move the ball out to either halfback wing.

The right halfback (***Player #4***) is the next player to receive the ball since he is not yet marked. In the meantime, the right winger (***Player #2***) moves to the right wing for a pass, as shown in **Stage 2**.

After the right winger (***Player #2***) receives the pass, he dribbles the ball back along the wing, as shown in **Stage 3**. In the meantime (***Player #4***), the original right halfback, now moves to a position at the right front of the goal waiting for a scoring opportunity (he must not go offside). The rest of the team also moves up field. **Player #2** turns and then makes the cross from his semi-rearward position to **Player #1**, as shown in **Stage 4**.

The Drill

- Set up the drill as shown in *Figure 6-9* (see previous page). Defending players are not used in this drill.

- Start the drill with a kickoff by the center forward *(**Player #1**)* passing the ball to the receiving right winger (***Player #2***), as shown in **Stage 1**. *Player #1* then moves up field to get into a scoring position.

- *Player #2* then passes the ball back to the center halfback (***Player #3***).

- *Player #3* passes to the right halfback *(**Player #4**)*.

- *Player #4* passes the ball up the wing to the right winger (***Player #2***), as shown in **Stage 2**.

- *Player #2* then dribbles *back* along the right wing.

- The right halfback (***Player #4***) overlaps the right winger by moving along the touch line and begins to cut in towards the center of the goal to possibly receive a pass, as shown in **Stage 3**.

- *Player #2* is now in position to make a Non-Blind Cross or a Blind Cross to *Player #1*, as shown in **Stage 4**.

- After three successful cross plays, repeat this drill by exchanging another group of forward players.

- If this drill is repeated at another time, run this drill on the opposite (left) side of the field.

- Run the drill for 15 minutes.

- **The coach is to observe that the players get the idea of the kickoff going initially backwards instead of forwards. They should also realize that, with a plan, a cross pass can occur indirectly from a kickoff.** *Note:* **During games, the players should not be permitted to override the coach under any circumstances and perform a kickoff in a different manner. If this occurs, it is strongly recommended that player get a prolonged period of bench sitting during games.**

Drill 6.9

SIDE-OF-THE-THIGH AND CALF TRAPS

(Run these two drills at different practices)

The Mechanics

The Side-of-the-Thigh Trap

The Thigh Trap is a useful trap for trapping balls arriving at the trapper, in the air just below waist level, while a player is at right angles to the plane of the trajectory. The trapping method is as follows: A ball is thrown rapidly overhanded to the player nearly parallel to the ground. The player is to align himself at a 90 degree angle with the plane of the trajectory and estimate the point of contact where the ball will meet the thigh. The player then lifts his thigh to a point that is approximately parallel to the ground while the knee is relaxed and bent 90 degrees. See *Illustration 6-2.* As the ball nears, the player must keep his eyes on it, following

Illustration 6-2.
The Side-of-the-Thigh Trap

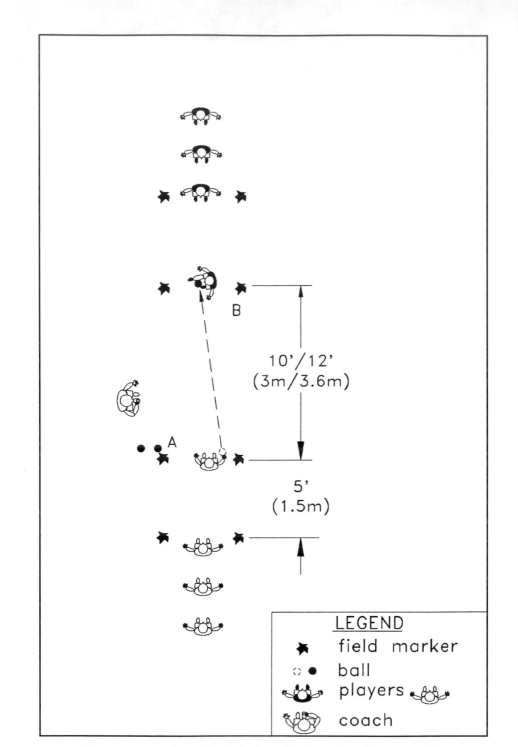

LEGEND

★ field marker
○ ● ball
players
coach

Figure 6-10. The Side-of-the-Thigh and Calf Trap Drills

it to the contact point on the inside of the thigh. As the ball makes contact, the leg is to recoil on impact to stop the ball from rebounding: It is important that the ball drops near the player. The player is to get control of the ball immediately, and dribble the ball a few feet (1 m).

The Drill

- Set up the drill according to *Figure 6-10.*

- The player at the head of one line is to throw the ball overhanded to the player at the head of the other line. The flight of the ball, as thrown at the trapper, needs to be near parallel to the ground.

- The trapper is to move to the ball, stop and turn 90 degrees, and wait for it to contact the side of the thigh. The ball should meet the player's right thigh at a point where the player can easily trap it.

- He is then to get control of the ball with the feet and dribble it for a few feet (1 meter).

- The player is to make three good traps with the right thigh. If the throws or traps are made badly, repeat the exercise until three good traps are made. The trapper and the thrower are to then reverse roles.

- After both players (the thrower and trapper) have completed three successful traps, they are to return to the end of their line to repeat the exercise with the left thigh when their turn comes up again.

- Run the drill for 15 minutes.

- **The coach is to observe that the player keeps his eyes on the ball at all times and that the ball drops dead near the player.**

The Calf Trap

The Calf Trap is a useful trap for trapping balls arriving in the air below knee level, while a player is at right angles to the plane of the trajectory. This trap is similar to the Side-of-the-Thigh Trap. The trapping method is as follows: The ball is thrown rapidly overhanded to the player, nearly parallel to the ground. The player is to align himself at a 90 degree angle with the plane of the trajectory and estimate the point of contact where the ball will meet the calf. The player then lifts his thigh so that the

Illustration 6-3.
The Calf Trap

soft calf tissue is aligned with the point of contact with the ball and that the knee is relaxed and bent. See *Illustration 6-3*. As the ball nears, the player must keep his eyes on it, following it to the contact point on the inside of the calf. As the ball makes contact, the leg is to recoil on impact to stop the ball from rebounding: It is important that the ball drops near the player. The player is to get control of the ball immediately, and dribble the ball a few feet (1 m).

The Drill

- Set up the drill according to *Figure 6-10* (see page 166).

- The player at the head of one line is to throw the ball overhanded to the player at the head of the other line.

- The flight of the ball, as thrown at the trapper, needs to be near parallel to the ground. The ball should meet the player's right calf at a point where the player can easily trap it.

- The trapper is to move to the ball, stop and turn 90 degrees, and wait for it to contact the side of the calf.

- He is then to get control of the ball with the feet and dribble it for a few feet (1 meter).

- The player is to make three good traps with the right calf. If the throws or traps are made badly, repeat the exercise until three good traps are made. The trapper and the thrower are to then reverse roles.

- After both players (the thrower and trapper) have completed three successful traps, they are to return to the end of their line to repeat the exercise with the left calf when their turn comes up again.

- Run the drill for 15 minutes.

- **The coach is to observe that the player keeps his eyes on the ball at all times and that the ball drops dead near the player.**

Drill 6.10

PASSING, GOALKEEPER TO DEFENSE

The objective of this drill is to start an attack by the goalkeeper via his defenders. This method of starting an attack by the goalkeeper is quite different from the unproductive method of kicking the ball up to the opponents' defensive area. This drill will familiarize the players with attacks that begin with short passes from the defensive area while reinforcing awareness for playing ball-possession soccer.

Whenever possible, the goalkeeper should throw or kick-pass the ball on the ground to the receiving player's feet, because by kicking the ball far up field there is only about a 30 to 40 percent chance of maintaining its possession. Since yardage gain is less advantageous than ball possession, the short direct pass is the most favorable activity for starting a new attack.

For the passing technique to be successful certain practices are mandatory. This drill requires the following:

- All players quickly get set for a rapid reintroduction of the ball back in play.

- The goalkeeper is to release the ball quickly.

- All players have the ability to trap and shield the ball under pressure.

- Only the goalkeeper takes goal kicks. When the goalkeeper comes in possession of the ball, all players are to quickly move into open spaces and no players are permitted to hang back to assist the goalkeeper in any manner or form.

The goalkeeper then wastes no time to get the ball to one of the defenders; preferably to one of the wing defenders. This activity will not take place without some initial consternation and errors, however, so it is best to initially employ this technique in all practices and the unimportant games. In addition, your opponents will rapidly become aware of this pass-off technique and begin to mark your players closely. When this occurs, the goalkeeper will have to mix in long goal kicks and punts. In time, however, there should be more frequent usage of the short pass by the goalkeeper as team confidence progressively develops.

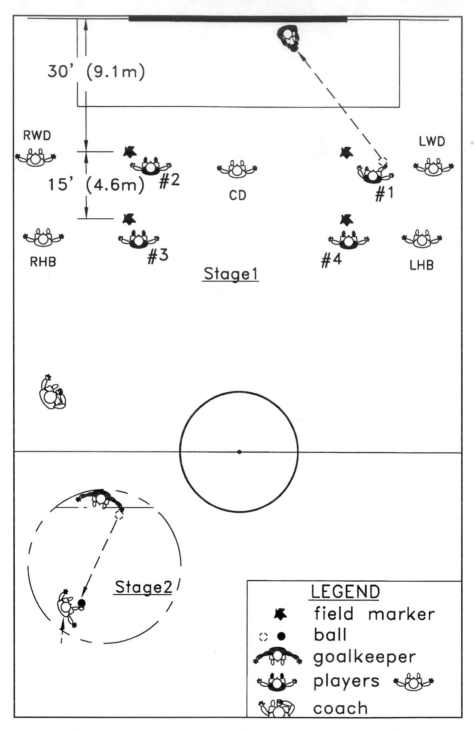

Figure 6-11. Passing, Goalkeeper to Defense Drill

This drill starts with a kick from an opponent (***Player #1***), as referenced in *Figure 6-11*. After this kick, the ball will be in the hands of the goalkeeper. If it is caught or grabbed by the goalkeeper, his next move will be to make a throw to a teammate (if the ball comes into his hands after first having crossed the goal line, the attack would be started by a goal kick). Both of these two conditions replicate game conditions with the exception of a goal being scored: A scored goal is not considered as a goal in this drill, the ball is to be reintroduced into play as if the ball was caught by the goalkeeper.

The initial defensive team consists of the goalkeeper and the light jersey players: There are three defenders and two halfbacks. When the goalkeeper gets possession of the ball, these players become the new offensive team as in normal activity. The opponents, initially on the attack, are the four players in dark jerseys: ***Players #1, #2, #3 and #4***. After the kick at the goal by ***Player #1***, the original attacking players (in the dark jerseys) go on the defensive. These opponents are then to mark the goalkeeper's teammates—the center defender (**CD**), the left wing defender (**LWD**) and the two halfbacks (**RHB** and **LHB**), thus leaving the right wing defender (**RWD**) open. This person is to receive the ball from the goalkeeper whether via a throw or goal kick.

The drill is started when ***Player #1*** takes a shot at the goal from the field marker located in front of the goal as shown in *Figure 6-11*. The goalkeeper will then collect the ball and launch an offensive by throwing (or kicking) the ball to the unmarked right wing defender. This unmarked receiver is to go to the ball, stop, trap and shield the ball (if necessary). He is then to pass it to any teammate (including passing it back to the goalkeeper) as one of the opponents moves to him (the opponents are free to move anywhere after the goalkeeper releases the ball).

The players in the light jerseys are to continue with the attack by dribbling and passing to teammates: Their movement is towards the bottom of the page in the figure. When the ball finally crosses the half-way line, a new attack is then to be restarted by ***Player #2*** moving over to replace ***Player #1***. All other players are to rotate in a clockwise manner.

The Drill

- Set up the drill as shown in *Figure 6-11*.
- ***Player #1*** is to kick the ball at the goal.

- The goalkeeper will collect the ball. He will then immediately throw or kick it to an open defending teammate in a light jersey (now on the attack), according to the rules described above.

- This teammate is to go to the ball to endeavor to trap (and shield it if necessary) before passing it to another open teammate.

- Each drill is over when the ball has been brought up to the half-way line or it is intercepted by the opponents.

- The full drill is over when all five light jersey players have had a chance at receiving the ball from the goalkeeper by rotating into the right winger defensive position.

- If other defenders have not been placed in this drill, it is important that they receive the same training, if not during this day's practice, at the next practice.

- **The coach is to observe that the ball is rapidly put into play and that the receivers go to the ball, shield it and then pass it to an open teammate.**

6b. Advanced Field Drills— Defensive

Drill 6.11
MONKEY IN THE MIDDLE

This is an extraordinary valuable drill when done correctly. Its purpose is to reduce player errors while reinforcing teamwork, shielding and safe passing. If you have performed the previous drill, you probably have observed from this goalkeeper passing drill that trapping, shielding and safe passing were full of errors. The methodology employed here will reduce errors and strengthen the players' abilities in the above three areas. The players will see and correct their own errors as they become the monkey in the middle of the triangle of players (or a square if there is an extra player). The drill is performed by having the players in the triangle pass the ball back and forth while the "monkey" in the center of the triangle endeavors to intercept it. The rules of this drill are strict and are reinforced by one's own teammates: For example, when the ball is passed by any of the players in the triangle, there is generally no choice as to who is to be the receiver, because the receiver is the player on the side furthest from the opponent. If an unsafe pass is made it will be obvious as it will be near the foot of the *opponent* = *monkey*. If the ball is touched by the monkey during a pass, the passing player has erred and moves into the monkey position. Any other offensive errors enabling the monkey to touch the ball will also cause this offending player to become the monkey. However, if no errors occur during two minutes of play, one of the players is to replace the monkey. The field of this drill is the enclosed area inside of the square formed by the four field markers.

The Drill

- Set up the drill as shown in *Figure 6-12* (see next page). If the square is either too small or large due to the age or size of the players, it

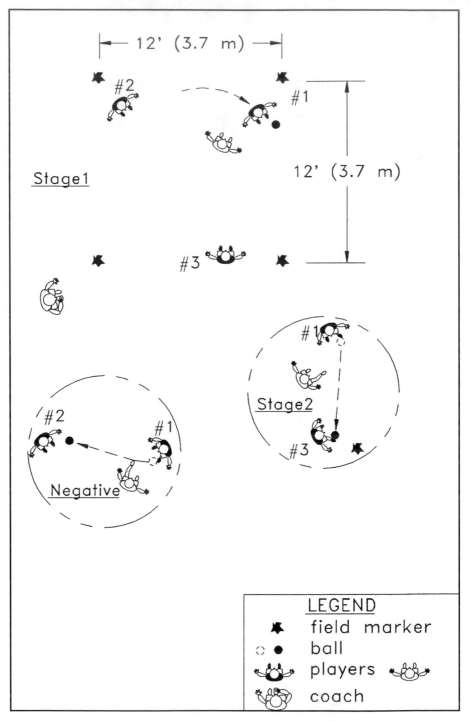

Figure 6-12. The Monkey in the Middle Drill

may be slightly decreased or increased. The drill will go ideally as
follows:

- *Player 1* will dribble the ball within the field markers as shown in
  Stage 1.

- The monkey (in the middle of the triangle) is to get possession. The
  player with the ball in this instance is *Player #1*. He passes it to
  Player #3. This is the only player that is clearly open for an
  unobstructed pass. This is shown in **Stage 2.** Note the *Negative*
  insert in *Figure 6-12*. In this instance, the ball should not be
  passed to *Player #2* as he is not in an ideal position for an
  unobstructed pass.

- This receiving player is to trap and shield the ball and dribble it. In
  this case it is *Player #3*.

- The monkey is to intercept the ball or deflect it. If he does not
  intercept or deflect the ball in two minutes, he is to exchange
  places with one of the other players.

- This drill is to run for 15 minutes.

- Repeat this drill often.

- **The coach is to observe that the ball is trapped near the player,
  shielded and passed safely, but generally she is to let the
  players apply the rules to their game.**

Drill 6.12
DEFENSIVE SCRIMMAGE

This drill is a limited scrimmage between a defensive team and an
offensive team. The scrimmage knits together the defensive principles
of this text into a team effort, but without the confusion that players
could experience by constantly oscillating between defense and offense
as they normally do in a game situation: This scrimmage requires players to either be always on defense or offense. In this drill, the cohesive
effort on the part of an offensive team is placed against the resistance
of a defensive team. This is not a continuous drill as it is to be restarted
each time the ball goes out of play or is caught by the goalkeeper. If it
is stopped by the coach, it can recommence at the place that the play
was stopped.

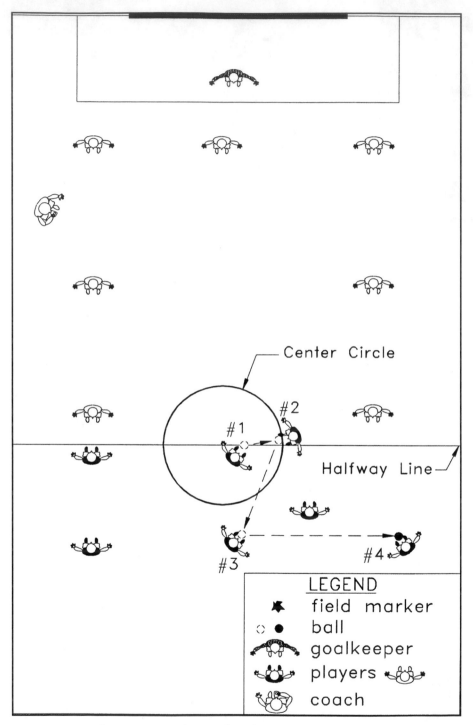

Figure 6-13. The Defensive Scrimmage Drill

The scrimmage begins with seven attackers. ***Players #1, #2, #3, and #4*** make a kickoff play precisely as described in Drill 6.8, Kickoff and Overlapping Wing Positions. The attackers are to attempt to proceed towards making the *cross kick* play as described in the above mentioned drill. Naturally though, with the defensive players being cognizant of that kickoff play, their resistance will be quite strong; however, the kickoff play should at least proceed as far along as with the wing halfback player (***Player #4***) receiving the ball. At this point, the offensive team may be forced to make a change in strategy (from the idealistic play described in Drill 6.8). After ***Player #4*** receives the ball, he may now pass it to any open available player. The scrimmage is then to continue, allowing the attack team to seek opportunities for scoring.

The job of the defensive team will be to mark each attacking player, especially the two forward wingers by staying goal-side of these players. The goalkeeper will have the opportunity to gain experience directing the defense and, if necessary, receive encouragement from the coach. The defensive team should thwart each and every attack by person-to-person coverage.

Note 1: The goalkeeper is the team's defensive director from this point on in his soccer career, if he or she has not already taken on this responsibility.

Note 2: Each time that the ball goes over the goal line, the touch line or is caught by the goalkeeper, a new kick-off is restarted by the attack team; unless the play went well up to that point and the coach prudently decides that the play should continue or be restarted from the point where the error was committed.

The Drill

- Set up the drill as shown in *Figure 6-13*.

- Start the drill with a kick-off.

- ***Players #1, #2, #3***, and ***#4*** are to proceed with the kickoff play as previously practiced in Drill 6.8, in order to make the cross pass or at least move this kickoff play along up to a point where ***Player #4*** can take advantage of other unguarded players' possible opportunities for scoring.

- The defenders are to defend person-to-person by backing up with their opponents: This defense should take place in the defensive one-third of the field.

- After four successful scrimmage drills, change the players around as needed to give players a chance to play different roles. Changing players to the different teams should also occur.

- The full drill should last for 30 minutes.

- **The coach is to stop the scrimmage when the play gets sloppy or mistakes are made. An explanation should then be given as to why play was stopped, then resume the play.**

Drill 6.13

Standing Block Tackle

The Mechanics

This drill is designed to teach the use of the Standing Block Tackle as well as to emphasize when not to employ it. The Standing Block Tackle is used to remove the ball from a dribbling player when a player makes a dribbling mistake and loses control of the ball. But, as mentioned many times throughout this text, a defender must not try to dislodge the ball from a dribbling opponent while it is under the control of the dribbler. However, should this player lose control of the ball and

Illustration 6-4. The Block Tackle

the defending player can get one foot in front of it as the dribbler tries to pass, the Standing Block Tackle can be successful. That is, it can be successful provided that the foot can present a sturdy obstacle in the ball's path. *Illustration 6-4* shows this blocking movement.

The move is as follows: A defending player is backing up with the dribbling opponent. The opponent suddenly loses the slightest control of the ball while she tries to pass the defender. The defender then places one foot (leg and ankle) in front of the ball and plants it firmly on the ground, having immediately shifted his body weight to this foot. As the defender pushes

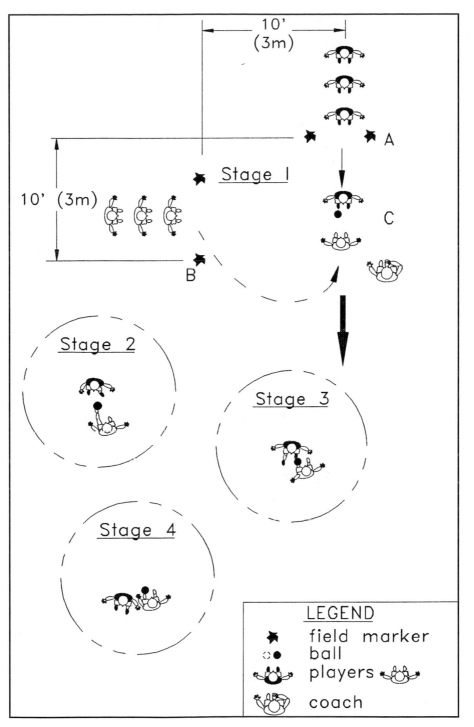

Figure 6-14. The Standing Block Tackle Drill

against the ball, the dribbler finds that it cannot move forward, but the momentum of her body then carries her forward passed the ball. With the foot remaining stationary against the ball, the defender ends up with it.

Note: It will be necessary to artificially allow the tackle to be made. For the defender to end up with the ball, the attacker will have to purposely move past the defender slowly and allow the tackle. Also, it is not likely that a few tackles tried in practices will be sufficient to make this move immediately successful; but with the mechanics being demonstrated, the players will eventually learn to apply the steps necessary for making successful tackles.

The Drill

- Set up the drill according to *Figure 6-14* (see previous page).
- The first player in line dribbles the ball from Location A toward C. This is **Stage 1**.
- The defender moves out from the line at Location B and also moves towards Location C, approaches the dribbler and backs up with her.
- The dribbler is to now attempt to pass the defender on the defender's left side (the dribbler's right side). As the dribbler slowly (for the purposes of making the tackle) places the ball to the defender's left, the defender places his left foot out in front of the ball to block its forward movement. This is **Stage 2**.
- The defender then shifts his weight onto the left foot to stiffen the resistance. This is **Stage 3**.
- The defender must hold the ball firmly in place with his foot as shown in **Stage 4**.
- After the dribbler moves past the ball, the defender pushes the ball forward and dribbles it for a few seconds. Both players then join the opposite line from which they emerged.
- The drill is to be 15 minutes long.
- **The coach is to observe a good tackle. If the defender does not end up with the ball, repeat the drill with the attacker slowing her movements further to allow a tackle to be made. The coach should also observe that the tackles are made only when the dribbling player loses control of the ball; for this drill the dribbler is to move slowly (but may not make any mistakes) to allow the tackle to be made.**

Index